BENEATH THE BLACKWATER
ALLIGATORS

NORTHWORD
WILDLIFE SERIES

Photography © 1996: Stan Osolinski/Dembinsky Photo Associates, Cover, 50-51, 68-69; William H. Mullins/F-Stock, Inc., 1; Tom & Pat Leeson, 4; Thomas C. Boyden, 8-9, 112, 122; Art Wolfe, 10-11, 16-17, 26-27, 76-77, Back Cover; Jim Brandenburg/Minden Pictures, 14-15; Mark J. Thomas/Dembinsky Photo Associates, 18-19,110-111; Du Zequan/China Stock Photo Library, 20-21; Lynn M. Stone, 22-23, 28-29, 30-31, 44-45, 78-79, 80-81, 88-89, 125; Melissa Farlow/National Geographic Society, 24-25; John Giustina/The Wildlife Collection, 32-33, 42-43, 128; Raymond K. Gehman, 34-35, 52-53,117; Michael P. Turco, 36-37; Joe McDonald/Bruce Coleman, Inc., 38-39, 126; Len Rue Jr., 40-41,86-87, 120; Stephen & Michele Vaughan/Vaughan Photography, 46-47; John Shaw, 48-49; Henry Holdsworth/The Wildlife Collection, 54-55; Gavriel Jecan/Art Wolfe, Inc., 56-57; Fritz Polking/Dembinsky Photo Associates, 58-59; Kent A. Vliet, 60-61; Jeff Simon/Bruce Coleman, Inc., 62-63, 84-85, 98-99; Wendell Metzen/Bruce Coleman, Inc., 64-65; Erwin & Peggy Bauer/Bruce Coleman, Inc., 66-67; Chris Johns/National Geographic Society, 70-71; Sullivan & Rogers/Bruce Coleman, Inc., 72-73; Richard Day/Daybreak Imagery, 74-75; Joe McDonald/Tom Stack & Associates, 82-83; Michael Francis/The Wildlife Collection, 90-91; CC Lockwood/Bruce Coleman, Inc., 92-93; Charles Melton/The Wildlife Collection, 94-95; John Elk III/Bruce Coleman, Inc., 96-97; Clay Myers/The Wildlife Collection, 100-101; Alan & Sandy Carey, 102-103,106-107; John Eastcott/Yva Momatiuk, 104-105, 119; Tom Vezo/The Wildlife Collection, 108-109; Gary Meszaros/Bruce Coleman, Inc., 114.

Additional photo captions:
Title page, Okefenokee Swamp; Page 4, Lake Okechobee, Florida; Pages 8-9, Everglades; Pages 38-39, Everglades; Pages 110-111, Everglades; Page 126, Everglades; Page 128, Everglades.

NorthWord Press, Inc.
P.O. Box 1360
Minocqua, WI 54548

Cover design by Russel S. Kuepper
Book design by Amy J. Monday

For a free catalog describing our audio products, nature books and calendars, call 1-800-356-4465, or write Consumer Inquiries, NorthWord Press, Inc., P.O. Box 1360, Minocqua, Wisconsin 54548.

Library of Congress Cataloging-in-Publication Data
Sleeper, Barbara.
        Alligators : beneath the blackwater / by Barbara Sleeper.
                p.   cm. -- (wildlife series)
        Includes bibliographical references.
        ISBN 1-55971-570-7 (sc)
         1. American alligator. 2. Crocodilia. l. Title. II Series: Wildlife series
QL666. C925S58 1996
579.98--dc20   96-11571

Printed in Singapore

BENEATH THE BLACKWATER
ALLIGATORS

Barbara Sleeper

NorthWord

NORTHWORD PRESS, INC.
Minocqua, Wisconsin

Dedication

To my wonderful children, Kelly, David and Josh,
who helped explore the wild swamps of Florida
and Georgia in search of alligators

Acknowledgments

I would like to thank the following individuals whose expertise helped make this project possible: Gary M. Stolz, Chief Naturalist, U.S. Fish and Wildlife Service; George R. Zug of the National Museum of Natural History, Smithsonian Institution; Jeffrey W. Lang, Department of Zoology, University of North Dakota; James Perran Ross of the Crocodile Specialist Group, University of Florida; Kent Vliet, Department of Zoology, University of Florida; Frank Mazzotti, Department of Wildlife and Range Sciences, University of Florida; Tim Gross, Department of Biotechnology, University of Florida; Ted Joanen and Ruth Elsey with Louisiana's Rockefeller Wildlife Refuge; Allen Woodward, Jeff Ardelean, Paul Moler, Harry Dutton, and Mark Trainer with the Florida Game and Freshwater Fish Commission; Peter Quincy with Florida Power and Light; Walt Rhodes, South Carolina Department of Natural Resources; and James Laray of Everglades National Park. I am most indebted to the numerous research scientists who have brought so many interesting crocodilian facts to light, and I take full responsibility for any misinterpretation of those facts presented in this text.

Special thanks go to my literary agent, Jeanne Hanson, for arranging the opportunity to write about alligators; and to *Animals* editor Joni Praded of the Massachusetts Society for the Prevention of Cruelty to Animals for the original magazine assignment that initiated my fascination with alligators.

Encouragement from special friends and family also makes a writing project such as this possible. One such friend is sweet Susan Heyward of Greenwood, South Carolina, who I first met 30 years ago in Florida over a baby alligator. Others include my creek-exploring, skull-collecting childhood chum, Marilyn Hedges; and horseback riding pal Gail Merrick, who introduced me to my first wild alligators. And special thanks go to my gardening buddy, Richard Nesting, whose quarter-century of ribald humor has provided both joy and inspiration.

Special mention goes to my "rotten little brother," Bill Sleeper, whose sibling pranks while water-skiing, aerial gliding, and gift-giving helped perpetrate my fascination with reptiles. He atoned for this childhood trauma by marrying Lynne Evans, the best jet-flying, horseback-riding, gallery-cruising sister I could ever hope to have. Most importantly, I would like to thank my positive, love-life parents, Norma and Bill Sleeper, for enthusiastically participating in everything from a large menagerie of childhood pets (with numerous escapees), to alligator searches in the reptile-infested swamps of the Okefenokee.

Heartfelt thanks go to Managing Editor Barbara Harold, Editor Laura Evert, and the entire staff at NorthWord Press, Inc. for contributing their unique skills and commitment to the completion of this project.

Table of Contents

Relic From the Past

Baby alligators, Everglades National Park, Florida.

The American alligator is a living relic from

prehistoric times. One of the largest alligators on record was killed this century at Apopka, Florida, in 1956 and measured seventeen feet, five inches. In 1879, an alligator killed at Avery Island, Louisiana, reportedly measured eighteen feet, three inches. The biggest gator on record, however, was killed in Louisiana in 1890 and measured nineteen feet, two inches. Today, a thirteen-foot alligator is considered large.

In the United States, the alligator has endured a history of persecution and poaching, but finally, protection. Approximately 20,000 alligators now live in Everglades National Park; and about a million in all of Florida. An estimated 1.5 million more live in the swamps, lakes and man-made canals throughout the rest of the coastal plains of the Southeast. Research into the behavioral ecology of these smart, adaptable, extremely social reptiles continues to shed light on the possible behavior and natural history of their extinct relatives—the dinosaurs.

People react strongly to alligators. Whether real or imagined, they hold one's attention. Topped with rows of protruding scales, their undulating, serpentine tail hints dinosaur. Their intelligent, predatory eyes, lethal jaws and secretive ways haunt, intrigue and scare.

Throughout the ages, these reptilian carnivores have been hunted, worshipped, feared and tamed. Among Native Americans, many Gulf Coast tribes developed songs or dances about the alligator and many ate their meat. The teeth and bones were fashioned into awls and vials, and the teeth were worn around the neck on leather thongs to prevent illness and poisoning. Some tribes used alligator skins to make ceremonial drums. Others wove an intricate "alligator entrails" pattern into baskets made with river cane and natural dyes. At Grand Lake, Louisiana, Native Americans constructed a 700-foot-long effigy mound in the shape of an alligator.

The legends of fire-breathing dragons may also be crocodilian-based. In China, the alligator is called *tulong* or "earth dragon." Early Chinese alligator myths may have spawned tales of the flame-throwing dragons.

A full-grown alligator is an impressive beast—complete with scales and spiked tail. It wouldn't take much to transform one into a fire-breathing dragon. For instance, on a damp morning in the Everglades, thousands of golden orb-weaver spiders bejewel the sawgrass marshlands with webs etched in dew drops. Amidst this fairy tale setting, alligators appear to breathe smoke. Bellowing to their nearest neighbors, the gators emit vapor from their nostrils. With a short spin of the imagination, such scaly beasts could easily have become the fire-breathing dragons of old.

Numerous unproved superstitions still persist about the magic, medicinal powers of swamp creatures. Have an itch? Cover the area with a cottonmouth snake's skin. Need a sure cure for rheumatism? Fry a toad with a dash of red worms, and eat them. Better yet, if rheumatism has got you down, just rub the aching limb—with some alligator fat.

In North Carolina, impotent male settlers were advised to eat the teeth of an alligator's right jaw to rekindle the flames of passion. The ashes from burned alligator skin soaked in oil were supposed to have narcotic effects. From the use of alligator oil for superstitious medicinal applications to the use of the gator's soft belly skin to upholster Victorian sofas, our native reptile has had a colorful, and at times bizarre association with us.

For example, in 1858, hot air balloonists Morat and Smith made a much publicized ascent over New Orleans, standing on the backs of two eleven-foot alligators. A week later they released an alligator tied to a parachute from an altitude of 5,000 feet.

When a thirteen-foot, 900-pound alligator named "Old Hardhide" died in 1985, the residents of Ponchatoula, Louisiana gave their beloved town mascot a royal sendoff: a horse-drawn hearse carried the dead reptile in a custom-designed casket followed by a jazz band and two thousand "mourners."

"Americans have found an astounding number of ways of integrating the alligator into their lives," wrote Vaughn Glasgow of the Louisiana State Museum. "It has become symbol, totem, medicine, mascot, pet, handbag, saddle, main dish, hors d'oeuvre, nightmare and souvenir. Every segment of U.S. society has been touched in some way by the alligator."

HISTORY OF AN ANCIENT REPTILE

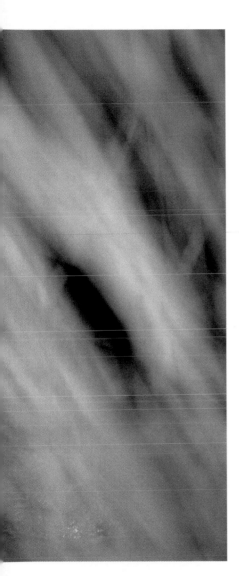

chapter 1

Everglades
National
Park, Florida.

*A*lligators have survived for millions of years,
little changed from the days when dinosaurs roamed the earth. Armed with sharp
conical teeth, muscular tails and tough, scaly skin, they are smart, efficient predators
that have weathered continental shifts, cooling climates and waves of evolutionary
adaptations and extinctions. As living fossils passed down from prehistoric times,
these relics from the past are remarkable for their tenacity. They are the planet's
largest living reptiles—surviving relatives of the extinct dinosaurs, huge

flying reptiles, and gigantic fish-like reptiles that once dominated the primordial swamps and seas.

Part of their success can be explained by their anatomy. More than two-thirds of their body mass is made up of skin and muscles. Their tough hide is composed of hundreds of rectangular scales. Bony plates, or osteoderms, embedded in the dorsal scales (or scutes) give them their armored look. Unlike modern reptiles, alligators and other crocodilians have diaphragms in their chest cavities and hearts that are designed for better blood circulation, more like those of birds and mammals. Their small—but remarkable—cerebral cortex drives a predatory intelligence that has enabled these smart, highly-adaptive reptiles to survive over millions of years.

Corkscrew Swamp, Florida.

According to evolutionary biologist Eric Buffetaut at the University of Paris, the long history of crocodilians is relatively well documented because the fossil record is so good. The aquatic habitats of most crocodilians were favorable to fossilization, as were those of terrestrial crocodiles, including an aberrant group of "hoofed" crocodiles. As a result, at the beginning of the nineteenth century, fossil crocodilians were among the first extinct vertebrates to be scientifically studied. They provided some of the earliest biological evidence for the process of evolution.

Like the dinosaurs, all crocodilians share the same family tree and early ancestry with a group of small, generalized reptiles called Thecodontia. They roamed the Earth 250 million years ago during the Mesozoic Era. Thecodonts averaged four to five feet in length including their tails, and had heavily armored skin and long, slender heads. Because their back legs were much longer than their front legs, paleontologists believe thecodonts were bipedal, like many of the dinosaurs that walked in an upright position.

Two pairs of large openings in the skulls of all modern crocodilians show their close ancestry to the dinosaurs. Called temporal openings, they are located immediately behind the eyes. Their function

is to accommodate the powerful muscles that open and close an alligator's jaw, providing a surface to which the muscles attach. The temporal openings make room for contracting muscle tissue as the jaws are slammed shut, and enhance the angular, ancient appearance of the crocodilian head. This unique system of double-paired temporal openings is a trait that can be traced back through the dinosaur fossil record to the thecodonts.

For millions of years, crocodilians shared prey and living space with the dinosaurs. In fact, a few large extinct crocodilians even ate them—until 65 million years ago when the last dinosaurs disappeared. Today, all crocodilians are grouped under the subclass Archosauria, a designation that aptly describes their ancient connection to the great "Ruling Reptiles." The big thunder lizards, giant plant-eaters, and flying reptiles "ruled" the planet for more than 150 million years, then were gone, leaving, among others, the crocodilians—and birds—to evolve as contemporary representatives.

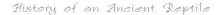

Early Relatives

Fossil evidence shows that crocodilians once came in all sizes. Some were small, averaging only twelve to twenty inches in length. Others were comparable in size to present-day alligators. A few were huge. An extinct Madagascar crocodile reached lengths of thirty feet or more. Even bigger was a six-ton crocodile that lived 75 million years ago called *Deinosuchus,* the "terror crocodile." It grew to lengths of forty feet and was thought to prey on dinosaurs. A gharial from the Pliocene (five to two million years ago) reached lengths of forty-five feet.

There were terrestrial crocodiles that hunted on land, some with six-inch teeth. Other enormous crocodilians cruised for prey in the primordial seas.

Not all crocodilians had the short, stubby legs typical of existing species. In 1877, Yale paleontologist Othniel Charles Marsh described a tiny, birdlike dinosaur from the lower Jurassic rock formations he called *Hallopus.* Due to academic rivalry, Marsh kept the location of his find secret. The only clues he revealed before his death about the location of the find were that it came from somewhere in Colorado, and was named after the *Hallopus* sandstone beds in which it was found. More than a century later, a geologist and two paleontologists combined detective sleuthing with modern analytical techniques to determine that Marsh's find came from a layer of rock located beneath a distinctive cone-shaped hill at an old quarry near Garden Park, Colorado.

As it turned out, Marsh made a couple of mistakes about *Hallopus.* Not only did it come from the upper Jurassic rock formations—meaning it was 150 to 160 million years old, not 200 million years old—but it wasn't a dinosaur at all. Taxonomic research conducted in 1970 revealed that *Hallopus* was a long-legged crocodile.

While the fossil record shows that ancient crocodilians enjoyed a remarkable adaptive variation in shape and form throughout a diversity of habitats, today's modern crocodilians are quite conservative in comparison. They differ from each other only in minor dental and osteological details—and in snout proportions—but little else.

In the waters of Big Cypress, Florida.

Modern Crocodilians

At present, twenty-three different species of crocodilians inhabit the planet's mostly tropical swamps and estuaries. They are all grouped under the order Crocodylia, which is divided into three separate families: true crocodiles; caimans and alligators; and gharials.

Gharials and the true crocodiles diverged from a common ancestor about 100 million years ago. Through geographic isolation, the gharial *(Gavialis gangeticus)* developed a long, slender snout and a multitude of sharp teeth for catching fish in the fast-flowing rivers of India and Nepal.

Chinese Yangtze alligators, Anhui Province, China.

The true crocodiles and alligators diverged from each other roughly 60 million years ago. This illustrates how variable the pace of evolutionary change can be. The separate, but parallel, lineage of alligators and crocodiles has endured longer than the time it took for the entire radiation of mammals to occur.

Even more interesting is the fact that birds, like dinosaurs and crocodilians, also have been placed in the subclass Archosauria. Much of crocodilian behavior today is very similar to that of birds. They build nests, invest energy in parental care, and call to their mates and young using special vocalizations to communicate between male and female, female and offspring, and offspring and adults. The young even form pods and follow their mother around like a brood of ducklings, often resting on her back.

Also like their avian relatives, crocodilians swallow gastroliths, or millstones. The debate continues as to whether these objects are swallowed intentionally to aid digestion, or are artifacts of indelicate ingestion. Worn smooth by gastric action and corrosive digestive juices, crocodilian gastroliths have taken the contemporary form of soda bottles, tin cans, bullets, jewelry, and marbles.

At present, there are only two living species of alligators in the world: the American alligator *(Alligator mississippiensis)*, and the rare Chinese alligator *(Alligator sinensis)* native to the freshwater marshes along the Yangtze River. Both species live outside the tropical zone inhabited by most crocodilian species, ranging as far north as the 40th parallel. In fact, the northern range of the American alligator is demarcated along the 15 degree

Fahrenheit isotherm of minimal annual temperatures.

Although it is widely accepted that most crocodilians are primarily tropical species, the gharial inhabits cold, glacial melt streams in Nepal; the broad-snouted caiman lives in temperate areas of southern Brazil and northern Argentina; Nile crocodiles occur in areas or at elevations where freezing temperatures occur annually; and mugger crocodiles also occur outside the tropics in India. Even so, severe winters sometimes kill American alligators that live near the northern extreme of their temperate range.

The only other members of the alligator group are several species of caimans native to Central and South America. They differ from alligators in the structure of their scales. Caimans have a greater number of keeled, plate-like scutes in the skin behind the head, which gives them a more armored appearance. They also lack the bony membrane in the nasal part of the snout found in alligators.

Today, an introduced population of spectacled caimans *(Caiman crocodilus)* shares habitat in southern Florida with the endemic American alligator and American crocodile. Escaped, or released as unwanted pets, these feral reptiles native to northern South America are quite content in the man-made canals near Homestead, Florida.

Alligators Today

Millions of alligators once inhabited North America's southeastern swamps and coastal areas. When the first Spanish explorers reached the New World and encountered *Alligator mississippiensis*, they named it *el lagarto*–the lizard. The word alligator probably evolved from that early usage.

In 1826, while surveying the banks of the Red River near its confluence with the Mississippi, John James Audubon met alligators in memorable numbers. In a scene reminiscent of the piles of Nile crocodiles that once edged East African rivers, Audubon wrote: ". . . they could be seen along the shores by the hundreds, or on immense rafts of floating or stranded timber, the smaller on the backs of the larger, all groaning and bellowing like thousands of irritated bulls about to fight."

Up until three million years ago, alligator species still inhabited Europe until they were driven out by the cold. Just half a million years ago alligators

reached as far north as Maryland. Today, *el lagarto* is most abundant in the extensive coastal marshes of southern Georgia, Florida, Louisiana and parts of Texas. Here, the reptiles thrive with winter temperatures that rarely dip below 35 degrees Fahrenheit. In some Texas marshes an estimated one hundred gators share each square mile.

In lesser numbers, gators can also be found in the large shallow lakes, marshes, swamps, ponds, creeks and rivers of Alabama, Arkansas, Mississippi, southeastern Oklahoma and North and South Carolina. They are equally at home in fresh and brackish water, and show a high tolerance for poor-quality water. Even though alligators lack functional buccal salt-secreting glands which makes it possible for some crocodilians to tolerate a saline environment, alligators do occasionally venture into salt water for short periods of time.

Alligators in the Everglades.

Viewed from above, an alligator is a work of art and symmetry.

Its elongated head and snout are counterbalanced by its muscular, tapering tail. Rounded at the mid-section with reduced appendages fore and aft, a gator's body seems neatly divided into thirds. Symmetrical rows of raised dorsal scales run in artistic, parallel lines from the base of a gator's neck to the tip of its tail. Often these dorsal ridges are all that is visible behind the triangular head of an alligator as it serpentines through the water. Armored, alien, ominous, the hint of scales at the surface designates a reptile—a big, predatory reptile.

Adults usually take one of two shapes—either long and thin, or short and stocky. Captive alligators tend to be fatter and have broader heads because they spend more inactive time on land. Gravity acting on the sheer weight of their heads causes them to spread. When held captive with a pile of other gators, their dorsal scutes tend to get filed smooth after years of crawling over each other. Well-fed captive alligators may live fifty to sixty years or more. In the wild, thirty is a ripe old age for a gator.

Okefenokee National Park, Florida.

Despite their somewhat sluggish appearance, these lizard-shaped reptiles are no slouches on land. In addition to their lethargic waddles and belly glides down steep banks, alligators can run faster than people can over short distances by rising up on their hind legs in a "high walk" that is as startling as it is fast. The stately, crocodilian high walk is unique among living reptiles. It more closely resembles the walking posture of mammals than the sprawled gait typical of reptiles. Some smaller crocodiles can accelerate their running gait into a vertical bounding rabbit-like gallop of two to ten miles per hour, propelled by their strong hind legs. As a result, the predatory speed and meat-seeking intelligence of crocodilians should not be underestimated.

"The American alligator is as much a symbol of wild country in the Southeastern swamps as the grizzly is in the Western mountains," wrote Frank Sargeant in 1982. For most of us, the opportunity to see one in the wild, "doing it's gator thing," is a thrill. Like the star-filled skies at night, alligators serve as visual, tangible links to distant, rarely imagined worlds. Spiked and scaly, these Jurassic throwbacks help rekindle the dreams, fears and fascination of unfettered childhood. To gaze into an alligator's eyes is to know what it would have been like to be stalked by a meat-eating dinosaur.

ALLIGATOR
OR
CROCODILE?

chapter 2

Spectacled
caiman,
Venezuela.

𝒥n the very southern tip of Florida it is
possible to see both the endangered American crocodile *(Crocodylus acutus)* and
the American alligator in somewhat close proximity. Both species are the only
crocodilians native to the United States. The ability to differentiate between the
two is important in order to appreciate a rare sighting of an American crocodile.

Of the fourteen species of true crocodiles, the American crocodile is the
only species with a widespread distribution in the Americas. Its extensive range

includes the brackish coastal waters of Central America, northern South America, and much of the Caribbean, specifically Hispaniola, Jamaica and Cuba. Only its northernmost range encompasses the southern sub-tropical tip of Florida where it resides along the warm coasts from Fort Lauderdale to Sanibel Island, including Florida Bay and northern Key Largo.

Of all the crocodilian species, only the Indopacific, or saltwater, crocodile *(Crocodylus porosus)* and the American crocodile inhabit primarily estuarine environments. This makes osmoregulation, the maintenance of internal salt and water balance, especially important for both species. Thick skin helps prevent the loss of fluids, the kidneys concentrate nitrogenous wastes into uric acid, and special salt glands in the tongue help excrete excess salt. The less salt-tolerant young American crocodiles drink rainwater that pools on the surface of brackish water and even bite at raindrops.

American crocodile (left) and alligator (right), Everglades.

The best place to see American crocodiles in the wild is in Everglades National Park at West Lake, Coot Bay Pond, and on boat tours from the Flamingo Marina. A few years ago a nine-foot female croc took up residence in the J. N. "Ding" Darling National Wildlife Refuge on Sanibel Island. Breeding populations are protected in the cooling canals of the Florida Power and Light Company's Turkey Point nuclear power plant near Homestead, at Crocodile Lake National Wildlife Refuge on northern Key Largo, and along eastern Florida Bay in the Everglades. Where their range overlaps, American crocodiles and American alligators coexist peacefully.

Although all crocodilians share the basic body design, alligators differ from crocodiles in a number of ways. Alligators have broader heads and wider, more rounded snouts. A crocodile's triangular snout is distinctively slimmer and more pointed. Alligator nostrils have a space between them; crocodile nostrils are very close together.

When an alligator shuts its mouth, most of its teeth are concealed—those that are visible point down from the upper jaw, giving its owner a grinning, buck-toothed appearance. When a croc shuts its mouth, teeth from the upper and lower jaws remain visible, particularly the large, lower fourth teeth which jut up just back of the nostrils. Crocodiles average seventy teeth, alligators eighty.

Both alligators and crocodiles are cryptically colored to blend into the shadows and reflections of sunlight on water. Even the pattern of their scales seems to mimic the ripple of disturbed surface water as well as the geometric designs created by a variety of floating water plants. Seen from above, an alligator's black color helps camouflage it

against the dark water surface. Seen from below, their light-colored underbellies conceal them against the eye-blinding glare of the bright water surface. Such cryptic coloration is ideal for a silent, stalk-and-ambush carnivore.

Sunbathing crocodiles also seem to disappear on land. Like sunbleached driftwood they blend into the vegetation. Alligators are usually darker in color than crocodiles, but not always. One author poetically described an alligator's black hue "as the same color, texture and shape as exploded truck-tire carcasses found along the freeway."

Albino alligators have been reported in literature as mostly white with golden eyes and mottling. Rare leucistic alligators have occurred in Louisiana. According to Vaughn Glasgow of the Louisiana State Museum, these unusual pure white specimens "look like walking patent leather." They have normal dark eyes, but lack patterning of any kind.

American crocodiles are endangered throughout their range. In fact, due to the resemblance between the endangered American crocodile and the American alligator, the latter is listed by the state of Florida as a "species of special concern," and by the U.S. Fish and Wildlife Service (USFWS) as "threatened due to similarity of appearance [with other endangered crocodilians]." By law, it is illegal to tease, harass, molest, capture, kill or feed either species.

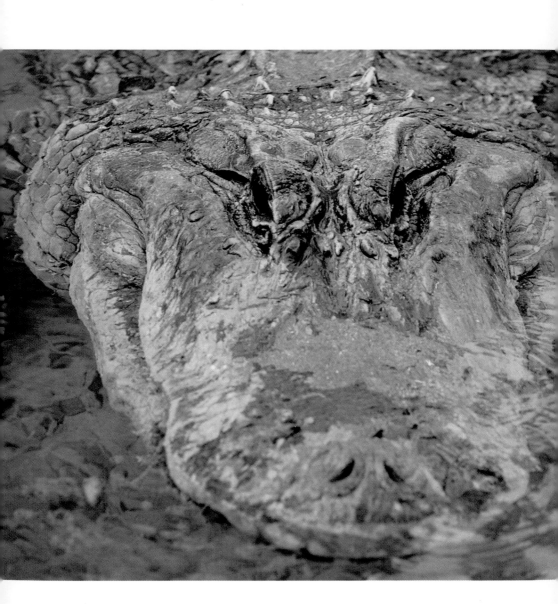

FOR THE LOVE OF WATER

chapter 3

Very old
American
alligator in
Everglades
National
Park.

The American alligator is an impressive

beast. With most of its body concealed underwater, an alligator's size can be deceiving. While the record length for an American alligator is nineteen feet, two inches, most adults average less than half that size. Only mature, old males may grow twelve to fifteen feet long and weigh up to 1,200 pounds.

Agile swimmers, these ancient reptiles tuck their legs close to their sides and propel their bodies forward with graceful sidestrokes of their muscular tails.

Their webbed hind feet serve as paddles and brakes, their tail as both motor and rudder. The vertically flattened, oarlike tails propel adult alligators through the water at a cruising speed of just over one mile per hour. When in pursuit of prey, alligators can swim much faster over short distances. The powerful tails enable them to briefly hydroplane at the surface, or leap and lunge out of the water up to five feet in the air with incredible speed.

Everglades National Park.

These scaly, semi-aquatic reptiles are most at home in water where they can remain submerged for an hour or more. Webbed feet aid their locomotion through water and over the swampy terrain at the shoreline. Powerful tails propel them with grace through their aquatic habitat. So adept are they at moving with stealth through the water, that these "sit-and-wait" predators can surface and submerge with hardly a ripple. Like silent, reptilian submarines, they quietly surface, then sink ominously out of sight, leaving only a telltale stream of bubbles at the surface.

Alligators depend on lakes, rivers, ponds and swamps for their prey, and seek refuge in the water to avoid excessive hot and cold temperatures. In fact, water temperature determines gator habitat selection, usually in more shallow water, where an alligator can best maintain an optimum body temperature of around 89 degrees Fahrenheit.

As adaptations for a semi-aquatic lifestyle, an alligator's ears, eyes and nostrils are placed high on its head, much like those of a hippopotamus. Sensory lip scales are also positioned at waterline, making it possible for an alligator to see, breathe, hear, smell and taste with little more than the top of its head exposed at the surface.

Like a submarine preparing to dive, alligators also close their hatches. A semitransparent membrane, or third eyelid, called the nictitating membrane, covers their eyes, and folds of skin close over their ears. Muscles contract sealing the nostrils

shut, and the gator's throat closes tight, enabling it to open its mouth to catch and hold prey underwater without drowning. Also, like submarines, the hydrodynamically designed alligators can adjust their buoyancy, enabling them to walk and rest on a muddy pond bottom as easily as they can float at its surface.

When motivated by fear, food or aggression, alligators can swim in short bursts faster than a person can paddle a canoe. Floating inconspicuously at the surface one moment, then sinking quietly out of sight the next, alligators are artists of illusion—concealing not only their presence, but their size.

"It seems a fitting paradox that such a heavy, lumbering animal should live under a blanket of one of the world's smallest and most delicate flowers," wrote nature writer Diane Akerman, describing an alligator's nose and bulbous eyes surfacing through the duckweed of a pond. The fragile plants not only provide cover for the reptiles, but a layer of vegetative warmth on windy days.

In Search of Warmth

Like all reptiles—including snakes, lizards and turtles—crocodilians are cold-blooded. This means that all of a gator's activity, including feeding behavior, metabolic rate, even digestion, is ultimately dependent on external temperature. For example, feeding behavior ceases when water temperatures drop below about 60 degrees Fahrenheit. All crocodilians need heat from the sun to activate digestive enzymes. Cold temperatures can kill a gator with a full stomach, as the food will rot instead of digest.

While warm-blooded animals regulate their body temperature internally, through metabolism, most cold-blooded

Bellowing gator, Payne's Prairie Preserve, Gainesville, Florida.

creatures have no such control. Instead, they must rely on external environmental conditions, and variable exposure to them, to warm up or cool down.

While an alligator's preferred activity appears to be dozing in the sun, it is the need for warmth to facilitate digestion that drives this behavior. Alligators often rest with their jaws wide open. Such gaping behavior is believed to have multiple functions. Evaporation from the moist lining of the mouth may possibly prevent the heavy-skulled head from overheating as the rest of the body is slowly warmed. Like a built-in fan, the in-and-out movement of the throat skin circulates cooler air around the head.

It has also been proposed that alligator gaping behavior serves as a social signal. It may also serve a health function. The tongue and inside surface of an alligator's mouth are covered with sensory papillae. By periodically drying out the mouth, sensitivity may be maintained while potential fungal or bacterial infections are held in check.

According to naturalist Connie Toops, on cool mornings, during the spring and fall, alligators crawl out of the water after sunrise to warm in the sun. Their

dark skin quickly absorbs the heat. When they get too warm, they return to the water to cool off, often repeating the process several times during the day. Whether sprawled across a log or basking on a bank, the sunbathing alligators typically return to the water by dusk, when air temperatures begin to drop. On cool windy days, or hot summer days, they remain in the water.

An alligator's vascular system plays an important role in thermoregulation. When sunbathing, increased blood flow to the skin maximizes heat absorption, as does its black coloration.

Another aspect of their physiology that has long intrigued scientists is their ability to remain underwater for an hour or more. To better appreciate this feat, just hold your breath and swim one pool-length underwater. Unless you are in terrific shape, just about every cell will scream for oxygen by the time you reach the far side.

Alligators have four-chambered hearts, like those of mammals, yet they can do something that we can't. When submerged, they can reroute their blood to reduce circulation to the lungs.

Loxa-hatchee National Wildlife Refuge, Florida.

N. Hennakao Komiyama of the Medical Research Council in Cambridge, England and his colleagues discovered that when crocodilians hold their breath, carbon dioxide builds up in their blood, dissolves, and then forms bicarbonate ions. The ions then bind to amino acids in the reptile hemoglobin. Once bound, the ions cause the oxygen-carrying hemoglobin to release additional oxygen molecules into the blood system. This biochemical reaction increases the amount of oxygen available to the reptile's body tissues when no external source is accessible. Compared to people, crocodilian hemoglobin unloads oxygen with super efficiency.

Such oxygen conservation is also enhanced by an alligator's behavior. These remarkable reptiles economize on energy expenditure whenever possible. Wasted motion, whether in the water or on land, is not part of their habits. By remaining immobile, they not only conserve metabolically, but remain unobtrusive—ideal behavior for a deadly predator.

According to Vaughn Glasgow, "The mysterious gloom of an alligator-inhabited swamp, coupled with the antediluvian appearance of the animal itself, have made the alligator a symbol of the netherworld in both literary and visual imagery." While enthusiastic herpetologists might disagree with this categorization, there is something definitely haunting about an alligator swamp. Especially when you know that the large, meat-eating reptiles are there, but invisible. Even more so, if you don't.

WHAT'S FOR DINNER

*Alligator
with a nutria
it has
caught.
Everglades.*

Alligators are, indeed, formidable predators.

It has been said that at sometime in their lives, they will eat every kind of living thing that comes within range of their jaws. In fact, anything that moves and is of manageable size is considered fair game by an alligator.

Keen Eyesight

Shine a flashlight across an alligator swamp at night, and you'll be amazed at the number of eyes that shine back. A swamp that appeared deserted by day is suddenly teeming with night life. A symphony of frog and insect calls fills the humid air against a backdrop of mysterious plops and splashes.

Young alligator in the Everglades.

Like cats, crocodilians have a thin layer of special reflecting tissue behind each retina called the *tapetum lucidum*, or "bright carpet." The tapetum acts like a mirror to concentrate all available light during the darkest of nights. This adaptation is an advantage for a night-active meat-eater that needs to see better than its prey. It is also what causes the alligator's haunting, coal-red eyeshine at night when caught in a flashlight beam. They shine back red, instead of white or yellow like other animals due to the specific reflective qualities of the gators' tapetum.

Alligators have intriguing, bulbous black eyes. Like all major predators, they must have acutely receptive senses in order to detect and capture their prey. Positioned as they are, crocodilian eyes provide twenty-five degrees of binocular vision, which makes it possible for them to judge distance and attack with accuracy. At night, with pupils fully dilated, their visual acuity has been compared to that of an owl's.

To protect their all-important eyes from injury—when threatened, attacking prey, or fighting—alligators can pull their soft eye orbits down into their skulls, letting them pop back up when the coast is clear. Before the eyes are lowered, the nictitating membranes close front to back, then the eyelids close top to bottom—then down periscope.

Alligators have another special visual

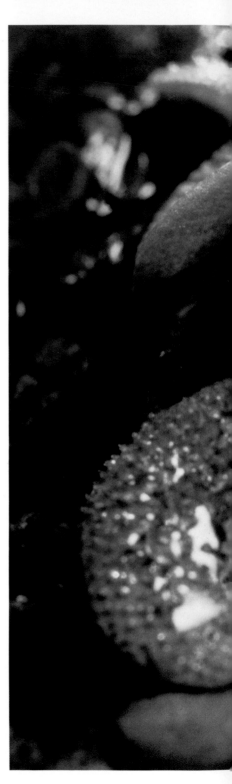

adaptation ideal for a sight-oriented predator. Like a compass
needle pointing perpetually north, a gator's oval-shaped pupils
remain vertical to the horizon, even when the gator tilts its
head. This adaptation for enhanced, undisrupted vision is made
possible by compass-like movement of the alligator's eyeballs.
But it only works if the alligator remains somewhat horizontal.
Flip a gator upside down on its back, and its visual system—and
equilibrium—become disturbed. Such an animal is not "hypno-
tized" as some alligator wrestlers claim. Visually disoriented,
with its eyes unable to focus, the smart creature simply remains
motionless while it experiences vertigo.

Other Senses

Physical stimulation from the environment is needed to
trigger the sense of touch, sight and hearing. Chemical signals
trigger the sensation of taste and smell. The sides of an alligator's head are loaded with sensitive touch receptors. Sensitive lip
scales resting at waterline enable a gator to detect movement
and vibration from potential prey, mates, territorial rivals and
approaching predators.

Alligators have a well-developed sense of smell which
they use to detect prey, both living and dead. The nasal cavities
that open into paired nostrils at the tip of the snout are loaded
with olfactory nerve endings.

Smell also appears to play an important role in olfactory communication
Everglades
National
Park.
between gators, especially during the
breeding season. Male alligators secrete
musk from glands at the base of their tail
when they bellow. Two throat glands located under the
chin possibly play an important role during the head-rub-
bing phase of courtship. When captured or attacked, alligators visibly evert
these glands. That alligators respond to such chemical messages, or pheromones,
has been proven experimentally. The smell of alligator musk often lingers in the
air following an attack on large prey.

All crocodilians have an acute sense of hearing. Alligators are always on
the alert for prey-like sounds, especially when hungry. They show an unmistak-
able response to the faintest vibrations produced when a small animal jumps
into their pond, even as they impersonate driftwood.

All crocodilians are nocturnal, which means they dine most often from
dusk until dawn—but not always. Opportunistic is the operative word when
describing alligator feeding behavior. Many an animal has lost its life to a nocturnal gator by day.

Teeth

Armed with sharp, replaceable teeth used for seizing, holding and crushing their prey, and powerful tails for skilled movement, crocodilians catch their food through stalk and ambush. With lightning speed they can entirely engulf a small water creature—or leap out of the water to grab a leg or snout of larger fare. Special throat flaps enable them to catch prey above or below the surface without swallowing water.

Alligators have enormous mouths. This fact isn't readily apparent when a gator's jaws are shut in their characteristically toothy grins. Light-colored skin along the jawline highlights about two-thirds of their anatomical smile. It is only when a hissing gator opens its great toothy maw, that you realize their jaws can fly wide open, past their eyes, to the base of their necks. A thick, white tongue resides inside this meat-eating cavern.

Powerful muscles can slam the jaws shut with irrevocable force. It has been estimated that their jaws can exert pressure of up to 2,000 pounds per square inch. That makes it pretty tough for prey of any kind to escape. While the muscles used for opening the jaws are very weak, the muscles used to shut them are so strong that even the strongest human cannot open them once they have closed on something. Only a punch to the sensitive snout or a poke in the eye will sometimes get a startled crocodilian to release its grip.

"And what big teeth you have . . ." American alligators have roughly twenty pairs of inch-long teeth on each jaw (eighty total), which they routinely lose and replace throughout their lives. This is possible because their teeth are not permanently rooted like human teeth. Instead, the hollow, conical-shaped teeth are interstacked below the gum line. New teeth continuously push up from the sockets to replace the worn and broken teeth. During the course of a fifty-year life span, an alligator could potentially produce up to 6,000 teeth.

And not just alligators had use for their large hollow teeth. Writers describe finding the discarded teeth "like white shells on a swampy shore." Called "swamp ivory," gator teeth were used by early American colonists to hold gunpowder. Each tooth, often carved with artistic designs, conveniently held the equivalent of one musket charge. In the 1800s, alligator teeth were also polished, mounted in silver and sold in jewelry stores as infant pacifiers.

Stalking

Some species of crocodilians are extremely fast and agile—especially the man-eating crocodiles. They are superb at stalking prey. Invisible until the moment of attack, such crocodiles usually float out in the middle of the lake, scanning the shore for movement. Should they see you on shore, they submerge and swim underwater toward you, remaining concealed until the last possible moment when they suddenly charge out of the water, attack in an eruption of snapping jaws to secure a firm hold and drag you back into deep water. This is why tourists are advised not to ponder life or otherwise linger near the edge of lakes and rivers in many parts of Australia, Africa and Southeast Asia. To do so could cost a life.

Most people assume that alligators eat constantly, killing everything that comes within range of their slice-and-dice jaws. In truth, these cold-blooded reptiles eat infrequently, as little as once a week during the spring and summer—and sometimes not at all during the winter months. Unlike warm-blooded carnivores that require a constant supply of high-energy protein, to maintain their internal body temperatures and fuel their predatory lifestyles, alligators don't have this problem. Being cold-blooded imposes an entirely different set of fuel and energy requirements on them. In comparison to mammals, alligators are extremely energy efficient—they only take energy when they can get it, and avoid expending it unless they have to.

In the back country of the Okefenokee Swamp.

American alligators prey on freshwater fish, turtles, snakes, crabs, waterfowl, muskrats, raccoons and otters—and make hors d'oeuvres of snails, crayfish and insects. They also scavenge on carrion. Hogs, deer, domestic calves and black bears have also been reported on the alligator menu, as have dogs. If a mutt is captured while swimming across a gator pond, the predatory event is usually marked by a short canine yip, brief struggle and then silence as the dog is unceremoniously pulled beneath the surface.

Attracted to movement of any kind, hungry alligators are always on the lookout for prey. Once spotted, they begin a slow, silent approach toward their target, with only their eye sockets and nostrils exposed at the surface. For the final calculated stalk and ambush, they submerge below the surface and glide with serpentine stealth right up to the animal. In an instant the attack is over. The unsuspecting victim usually meets its quick end in an eruption of gaping jaws and thrashing tail.

Smaller prey is simply grabbed and dragged underwater. Larger prey may first be knocked off balance with a blow from the gator's massive tail. Once a firm jawhold is secured, the gator violently shakes its head back and forth to stun the animal and uses its powerful tail to spin and roll underwater. The conclusion is almost always the same—death by drowning.

Tails

All crocodilians are highly successful, opportunistic carnivores. They use their head and tail as battering rams for both escape and assault. A flexible backbone enables them to rapidly swing their jaws and body to left or right, and literally curl into a snout-to-tail doughnut shape. Propelled by their tails, these versatile hunters ambush terrestrial prey along the shoreline, lunge at waterfowl

and fish that pass too closely, and launch submarine attacks on edibles below the surface. Their muscular tails also enable them to leap vertically out of the water to snatch prey from logs and over-hanging branches.

Alligators also use their tails as part of visual displays to each other. During courtship and territorial contests, gators often raise their heads and tails out of the water. By doing so, particularly in contests of dominance, they are able to show off their true size.

"Dominant animals advertise their large size by swimming boldly at the surface," explains biologist Jeffrey Lang from the University of North Dakota. "A threatening individual inflates its body and assumes an erect, static posture to further exaggerate body size. Tail thrashing is often employed during aggressive encounters. On land, dominant animals move the tail from side to side just prior to attack. Sometimes just the tip is moved quickly back and forth."

A crocodilian tail is an impressive weapon. During a trip to Zambia's Kafue National Park, I learned how dangerous the tail can be when used during an assault. An eight-foot Nile crocodile had been hit and killed by a Land Rover as the reptile crossed a dirt road in the park. At the request of a photographer, I straddled the

Scales on the tail of an American alligator, Ding Darling National Wildlife Refuge.

large, dead reptile around its mid-section. As I began to sit down on the crocodile's back, its huge tail suddenly came alive and whipped my left leg in a reflexive sideswipe. Not only did it hurt, but my heart just about exploded out of my chest from the surprise. Individuals who have survived alligator attacks have described being first knocked off their feet by the tail.

Digestion

Lacking molars, gators can not chew their food. Instead, they shake and slap the carcass against the ground or water surface to rip off bite-sized pieces. They also tear off chunks of meat by rolling with the carcass. Crocodilians can dismember an animal by fastening their jaws into a muscle mass, or limb, and then spin in the water until a piece of meat or a joint is torn loose and then swallowed. Prey may be torn apart when two crocodilians grab it and roll in opposite directions.

To aid this process, alligators often let decomposition tenderize their food. Prey is sometimes stored in a gator's underwater den or dragged around in their mouths for several days until it rots enough to be eaten.

Alligator eating a garfish, Everglades.

A captured bird quickly becomes an unrecognizable species after being mouthed and shaken by a gator. When feeding, a gator raises its head above water, and with a characteristic jerk, tosses the meat to the back of the throat where it is gulped and gone—using gravity to speed the process.

In contrast, I once observed a smaller alligator gumming a turtle as egrets flew across the fiery orange sky to roost in Everglades National Park. Long dead, with its lifeless neck dangling from its shell, the turtle was not easily consumed. For more than an hour, the gator just lay there, motionless, dead turtle clamped firmly between its jaws. This alligator's feeding habits were very slow.

The J. N. "Ding" Darling National Wildlife Refuge on Florida's Sanibel Island is another excellent place to watch alligator behavior. During the five-mile loop drive through the refuge, our family spotted a large alligator with a dead raccoon in its mouth. It was apparent the gator had been holding onto its prey for quite a while, as the raccoon seemed far from fresh. The big reptile made no attempt to eat the bedraggled mammal, and paid little attention to the human spectators that gathered. It just lay motionless on the muddy mangrove bank, letting natural processes tenderize its prey.

Further down the road, another small crowd of visitors had gathered by

the roadside. The focus of their excited attention was a lone gator making a stealthy approach toward a flock of water birds bobbing offshore. Only the top of the gator's angular head, nostrils and alert eyes were exposed. Unlike the human observers, the birds remained oblivious to the approaching reptile. They flew and landed close to the predator, and paddled within snapable reach. Their constant movement brought first one bird, then another, too close to the gator—yet none were grabbed. The suspense and repeated close calls caused the binocular-toting visitors to gasp in anxious unison.

Floating about their ponds on carnivore patrol, alligators serve the same function as terrestrial predators. At the top of their food chain, they cull the weak, the diseased, the unwary. Their feeding behavior helps to maintain healthy prey populations. And as meat-eating scavengers attracted to the deceased and decomposing, they also help to recycle nutrients into the food chain.

COURTSHIP
AND MATING

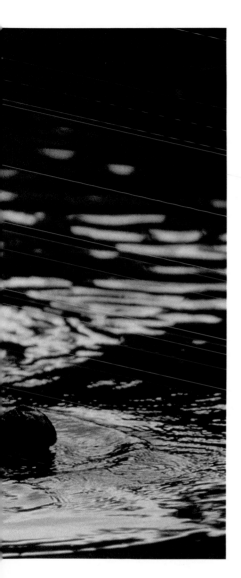

chapter 5

Alligators
mating,
Payne's
Prairie
Preserve,
Florida.

Spring is the season of love for the

polygamous alligators, particularly in Everglades National Park. With hormone levels elevated, gators go a courtin'. At this time of year, the swamps reverberate with their bellowing calls.

Courtship can be a testy time. Battles over territory can leave males wounded and dead. During such challenges, two males face off, glare at each other, hiss and lash their tails back and forth. The weaker male may concede immediately. More

evenly matched males usually hold their ground and fight.

The battles are intense. The water churns as the reptiles grapple and roll. On land, the rivals draw blood as they bite each other's head, limbs, tail and back. Combatants lose legs, even tails, during such fights. The victor often eats his rival. To see a big alligator with only a raw stump for a tail underscores the lethal nature of the fights.

Bellowing

Alligators communicate with each other using visual, aural, tactile and olfactory cues. Complex body postures and movement communicate a variety of information. So do secretions from the cloaca and paired glands located under the chin. Both sexes give off musk. In fact, after an alligator bellows, an oily sheen often surrounds the reptile in the water like an oil-slick.

According to Jeffry Lang, crocodilians are the "loud mouths" of the reptile world with the American alligators the most vocal "singers and talkers" of them all. Alligators hiss, grunt, cough, growl and bellow. Such vocal messages play a crucial role in the diverse and complex signaling system unique to crocodilians.

A long, loud, full-bodied alligator hiss is designed to make even the most courageous retreat. It works. This threatening sound is typically produced as a warning just prior to a defensive attack. Such a breathy response may also have contributed to the myths of fire-breathing dragons.

American alligator cannibalizing another, Everglades.

Bellowing choruses occur most often during the spring when breeding groups congregate. Usually performed in the early morning and late afternoon, the resonant choruses can last from ten minutes to more than half an hour. When produced by a mature male, the sounds can be intense. The repeated calls carry over great distances. Females also produce a single, characteristic bellow-growl when approached by a male. The tone and intensity of a gator's bellow is influenced by body size, gender and individualized differences in calling patterns.

Alligators are adept at manipulating their water environment for enhanced auditory and visual displays. As part of their social repertoire, they also blow air bubbles underwater and make loud popping sounds by rapidly opening and closing their mouths as they head-slap their lower jaws onto the surface, much like a beaver slaps the water with its tail. The males head-slap to threaten and show dominance, swishing their armored tails back and forth in the water as part of the display.

During his exploration of Florida two hundred years ago, naturalist William Bartram wrote, "The alli-gators were in such incredible numbers, and so close together from shore to shore, that it would have been easy to have walked across on their heads, had the animals been harmless." In the same romantic vein, he described his impression of these bellowing beasts. The collective sound "most resembles very heavy distant thunder, not only shaking the air and waters, but causing the earth to tremble; and when hundreds and thousands are roaring at the same time, you can scarcely be persuad-ed, but that the whole globe is violently and dangerously agitated."

Everglades National Park.

To bellow, a male alligator noticeably inflates as he raises his tail and head out of the water. Slowly waving his tail back and forth, the gator puffs out his throat, and with mouth closed, begins to vibrate the air. Just before bellowing, male alligators project an infrasonic signal at about 10 Hz through the water that causes vibrations in the ground and in nearby objects. The low-frequency vibrations travel great distances through both air and water to advertise the caller's presence. The vibrations are so strong, they literally make the water "dance" in a visual display of sparkling droplets that leap all around the back of the calling male.

At least ten different species of crocodilians, including alligators, perform "the water dance." In every case, it is only the males that perform it. They use it to woo females, and to signal location and dominance among other males. Some species do the water dance without bellowing. Male alligators routinely synchronize their water dances to a specific point in the rhythm of their calls. Some perform a whole medley of water dances, making the water leap and shimmer for twenty seconds or more.

In 1944, a biologist at the American Museum of Natural History made an

amusing discovery. Orchestra members played a variety of instruments to Oscar, the museum's resident alligator. Each time an instrument hit B-flat, Oscar launched off into a rumbling chorus of wild bellowing. And the response wasn't specific to Oscar. It turns out that all alligators are tuned to B-flat—it is the tone they hit when they bellow.

Planning a trip to the Everglades? You just might want to pack a B-flat pitch pipe, or your favorite French horn. Sonic booms, thunder and other loud noises also trigger spontaneous choruses of gator bellowing—as does spring, when hormones rise for courtship.

Alligator Amour

A crocodilian's reproductive cycle is the most advanced among reptiles. It is both protracted and complex. They show sexual dimorphism; sexual maturity is determined by both size and age; and all species lack sex chromosomes, relying instead on incubation temperature to determine gender.

Alligators reach sexual maturity when they are around six to ten years of age, or roughly six feet in length. Growth rates vary depending on temperature and food availability. In the northern part of their range, with shorter growing seasons, female alligators can take eighteen years to reach sexual maturity. Although both genders are identical in appearance, males grow faster and larger than females. Lacking secondary sexual features, there is no way to accurately determine the sex of a gator, except through manual inspection of the cloaca.

Crocodilian courtship behavior in the wild is still poorly understood due to difficulties observing the reptiles in their aquatic environments. Specific breeding patterns appear to vary with habitat. Contested male dominance hierarchies apparently influence male access to females.

According to Jeffrey Lang, male alligators form social groups or aggregates in lakes and open water canals during spring, similar to the seasonal formation of breeding leks in birds. Females travel to the males and courtship and mating takes place here. In other habitats, such as those with sink holes or rivers, alligator males go in search of females.

Adult and subadult males prefer deeper, open water where they remain year-round. Only occasionally do they venture into the more secluded, heavily vegetated

areas used by the females. Females usually have small territories, while males can occupy ranges greater than two square miles. Like the males of many species, male alligators roam more widely than females. In Louisiana, scientists tracked one adult male as he traveled through the marshes for thirty-three miles.

During the April-to-May courtship and breeding season, mature alligators seek open water areas. Within three to four weeks after mating, the females move into marsh areas to nest where they remain until the following spring. In Florida, all eggs are laid within a two-week period in June. With hormone levels elevated and courtship in progress, alligators are more aggressive than during the rest of the year. Yet courtship is typically slow and protracted.

Alligators court and mate in water. Courtship can last for several hours, and is thought to help synchronize both ovulation and spermatogenesis.

January in the Everglades.

According to herpetologist Kent Vliet at the University of Florida, the short, synchronized breeding season lasts just two months, but during that time the female is only receptive to sperm for a few days. Most males appear willing to court and mate throughout the breeding season and typically pursue the females. However, during a two-week period of heightened fertility from the end of April throughout the first two weeks in May, females turn the tables and aggressively pursue the males for copulation.

The amorous female gently pushes the male, rubs his head with her snout, nuzzles his neck and slides her body over his. She may even ride on his back. Her persistent pushing, bumping, rubbing and caressing usually works to get the male's attention, especially because so much of her contact is focused around his head, the sides of which are loaded with sensitive touch receptors. Once the male is activated, both partners engage in mutual snout and back rubbing, leading eventually to copulation.

In the early 1980s, when Kent Vliet couldn't collect enough data on gator mating habits by observing their behavior from shore, he simply jumped in the water with 150 of the scaly beasts at a breeding farm in St. Augustine, Florida. Crouching chest-deep in the water, Vliet got eye-to-eye with his research subjects in an effort to see the world from an alligator's point of view. He hoped to decipher the subtle body language and visual cues used during courtship.

Established in 1893 by George Reddington and Felix Fire, the St. Augustine Alligator Farm is billed as the oldest existing alligator farm in the world. In 1937, it was combined with another alligator farm in Jacksonville, Florida. The merger resulted in a collection of the largest, fattest, oldest alligators in captivity. It was here, in a shallow lake filled with more than 150 of these

ancient reptiles, most hidden below surface, that Vliet decided to go swimming.

One of the first things Vliet learned during his study
was to avoid swimming with the alligators in the morning
when the reptiles seemed more aggressive. He also learned
not to talk while in the water with the hefty reptiles—as
they didn't seem to appreciate human chatter. Should the
curious gators get too close, Vliet carried a big stick to pop
them in the snout. Differences in their markings—scars,
scales and bumps—eventually made it possible for Vliet to
recognize individual gators during the
course of his study.

*Male
and female
alligators
bellowing
together,
St. Augustine,
Florida.*

"Alligators are very curious animals," notes Vliet. "They are creatures
of a two-dimensional plane. Because
they can't see very well underwater,
one way they investigate a new object
is to bounce off it." According to
Vliet, when a 400-pound male starts
to bump a female gator a third his
size, you can feel it. Putting the
squeeze on each other seems to be an important part of
alligator courtship. They take turns body- pressing each
other, which enables them to assess the size and fitness of
their partner. The sense of touch is very important during
this process.

After a prolonged period of mutual rubbing and
caressing, during which the courting couple even blow bubbles at each other, the male puts his head over the female's
neck and presses her down. Embracing her with his fore-
limbs, he begins maneuvering his body around her for final
union—the goal being to join cloacas located under the
base of each tail. So joined, copulation lasts only two to
three minutes—a relatively short stint for a reptile.

It has been more than a decade since Vliet floated up
to his neck with alligators. He earned his doctorate and went
on to study the effect of stress-induced hormone levels on
alligator reproduction. It was a bold move to go eye-to-eye
with so many alligators. The fact that he survived repeated
dips in the carnivore pool helped put at least some of our
worst alligator fears to rest. His research also revealed a relatively gentle side to alligator mating—one quite touching
considering the armor, strength and weaponry brought to
such unions.

NESTING AND YOUNG

Alligator
nest
in the
Everglades.

$\mathcal{F}$rom late June to early July, about two
months after courtship has started, females begin to nest, building mounds of rotting grass in which to lay their eggs. After mating, the sexes have very little to do
with each other again until the following spring. Only the females build and guard
the nests and remain with their young.

Nest

Because flooding can kill developing alligator embryos within twelve hours, the nests are built on higher ground by the female. The exact location depends on a number of factors. Sometimes the same site is used year after year.

Rising three feet from the ground, with a diameter of about six feet, the nest mound looks like a strange igloo made of sawgrass and cattails. Built at the start of summer when it is both warm and damp, the mound of rotting vegetation is lined with mud. The nest location is determined by the female. Sometimes nests are abandoned before completion. Females occasionally take advantage of the reproductive efforts of other alligators by laying a clutch of eggs in their nest. Turtles also incubate their eggs in alligator mounds.

Baby alligator hatching in the Okefenokee Swamp, Georgia.

Using a hind foot to dig a conical depression in the top of the nest, a female lays twenty to fifty white eggs—about one every thirty seconds—in the egg chamber. She uses her hind feet to cushion the descent of each egg into the nest. The egg chamber is then covered over with more vegetation. The number of eggs deposited in the nest depends on the age and size of the mother.

Incubation

Incubation lasts approximately sixty-five days, during which the female remains close by, guarding the nest from predators with throaty hisses and threatening lunges. Raccoons, skunks and fire ants are the predominant egg stealers.

The female does not incubate the eggs herself, but instead, relies on the mulching effect of the nest material to generate heat. The decomposing plant material, in combination with the nest design, helps keep the nest cavity at a constant temperature.

Studies first reported in 1982 revealed that an alligator's gender is temperature dependent—determined by incubation temperature rather than genetics. Most crocodilians incubate their eggs at about 86 degrees Fahrenheit. temperature extremes below 81 degrees or above 93 degrees tend to kill the embryos of most species.

Among American alligators, nest temperatures of 90 to 93 degrees Fahrenheit typically seem to produce males, temperatures of 82 to 86 degrees produce females. Location of the nest as well as egg position within the nest cavity can influence gender. Whether or not a female

intentionally determines the gender of her offspring, influencing population sex ratios through choice of nest site, is now being studied.

Further research has shown that offspring incubated in a cooler nest seek out cooler living temperatures during life. Even the hatchlings' coloration is affected by temperature. Lighter-colored hatchlings emerge from cooler eggs, darker-colored hatchlings from warmer eggs.

Scientists have shown that temperature-determined gender occurs in many reptiles, including crocodilians, turtles and leopard geckos. Among sea turtles, warmer incubation temperatures produce females, cooler temperatures males. Among crocodilians, it is just the opposite.

Most importantly, knowledge about the species-specific parameters for temperature-dependent sex determination (TSD) gives conservationists a great tool with which to manage captive breeding programs. "Working with only a few eggs," says David Alderton, "it is possible to maximize the production of female offspring simply by adjusting the incubation temperature. For many of the endangered species, this offers great hope for their survival."

Hatchlings

Most baby alligators hatch in late summer from mid-August to mid-September during the rainy season. They announce their readiness to hatch with audible squeaks and grunts. Using a temporary "egg tooth," or caruncle, grown just for the occasion, the hatchlings cut their way out of their shells. Their

high-pitched calls alert the nest-guarding female of the long-awaited moment. To help free her young, she uses her front feet to dig into the nest mound, removing debris covering the eggs. She may even lift the eggs in her massive jaws, and help crack the shells by gently pressing them between her tongue and palate. Females are able to recognize rotten eggs, and simply swallow them during the hatching process.

Weighing about two ounces each, the eight-inch-long hatchlings are miniature versions of their parents. Only their coloration is different. Marked with bright yellow crossbands against a black background, the young gators rely on camouflage to reduce heavy predation. The striped pattern effectively conceals them against a background of swamp vegetation. As they mature, alligators lose the yellow banding and turn almost black.

Young alligator floating in the Florida Everglades.

Upon hatching, the young gators head for the nearest water under the watchful eye of their mother. An innate orientation response to the brightest horizon and presence of humidity helps them find water. The mother often carries her young to the safety of shallow water in her mouth.

Taking advantage of safety in numbers, the juveniles form a pod that remains near the mother as they forage for food. Should the pod or any individual young gator be threatened at any time, the guardian female will immediately come to their rescue.

In late summer, if you listen carefully during a walking or canoeing tour of Everglades National Park, you just might hear the faint grunts of alligator hatchlings sheltered in a sawgrass tussock. Should you happen to see one, never approach the little reptile, as its big, protective mother is sure to be close by, just waiting to hear the first faint strains of a distress call. In fact, any adult gator nearby will respond to such calls. It has been said that a juvenile alligator becomes an adult when it starts responding to distress calls instead of producing them.

Mother Love

Female gators show a level of maternal care uncharacteristic of most reptiles. Although the female does not incubate the eggs, she aggressively guards her nest. In the Everglades, nesting females have reportedly attacked small boats and

climbed onto an airboat.

During incubation, the female periodically rests her head across the fermenting mound to listen for audible signs of hatching. Upon hearing the faint grunts of her young, she digs open the nest. The female often helps transport the hatchlings to water in her mouth, and allows her yellow-banded offspring to crawl onto her back for rest and safety. This behavior is remarkable for a cold-blooded carnivore that, when given a chance, will often make a meal of another alligator.

For the first few days after hatching, baby gators survive on the nutritious remains of their embryonic yolk sac. Soon after, they must learn to fend for themselves, eating worms, insects, minnows, small crabs and tadpoles. As they mature, they add frogs and fish to their diets, then small mammals. Scientists estimate that about half of the protein eaten by rapidly growing immature alligators is converted to body protein. Under ideal conditions, young alligators can grow nearly a foot a year for the first three to four years of life.

Because alligators remain with their mother for two years or more, some females have been observed with the young of two broods—the newly hatched with yearlings that are twice their size. The young alligators remain in the area where they were hatched until they are two to three years old, then they disperse.

Baby alligators are vulnerable to many predators, including large fish, birds, bobcats, otters, snakes, raccoons and large alligators. Eighty percent will not

survive the first two years of life. Once an alligator reaches about four feet in length, they are relatively safe from predation, but are still vulnerable to cannibalism and poaching. Even so, crocodilians manage remarkable population comebacks when not hunted or harassed.

In fact, alligators appear to limit their population size to match niche availability. Social behavior, including dominance hierarchies and aggression levels, play an important role in controlling population growth. When too many gators are present, crowding causes stress levels to rise, which, in turn, causes testosterone levels to decrease. Under such conditions cannibalism increases, with increasing competition for food, territory and nest sites.

Reproductive Problems

Crocodilians have been compared to the shark, cockroach and fly in their ability to survive for eons. Scientists at the University of Florida have recently discovered a possible chink in their armor.

Since the 1980s, alligator, turtle and bass populations have been on the decline in Florida's third-largest freshwater lake, Lake Apopka, near Orlando. In twenty years, the lake's gator population had dropped from an estimated 2,000 to around 500. Because alligators are at the top of their food chain, scientists decided to investigate. Like humans, alligators are long-lived, which gives them a chance to accumulate contaminants in their bodies over time. The scientists discovered that pollution was definitely the culprit.

Baby alligator on its mother's back, Ding Darling National Wildlife Refuge.

According to University of Florida endocrinologist Tim Gross, fewer male alligators were being born at Apopka Lake. Their gonads not only appeared abnormal, but their production of reproductive hormones was also abnormal. Both male and female alligators showed elevated levels of estrogen; males showed reduced levels of testosterone.

In 1980 large amounts of the pesticide Dicofol were spilled into a stream that drains into the lake. Dicofol is made from the notorious "endocrine disrupters"—DDT and its derivative, DDE. Both cause hormone imbalances that result in reproductive problems. Ongoing contamination from agricultural pesticides continues to pollute the lake. Although the alligator population at Lake Apopka has begun to recover, the study serves as a warning for more widespread environmental problems, with long-term health implications for people as well as wildlife.

HOME
SWEET HOME

chapter 7

Everglades
National
Park.

*A*lligators play an important role in the
ecology of their ecosystems, particularly in the Everglades. In fact, their presence
there is critical to the seasonal cycles of wildlife and habitat. They modify their
environment to provide gator-made wildlife refuges that are used by other animals, especially during the dry season.

Gator Holes and Dens

South Florida typically experiences a dry season during winter and spring, followed by heavy rains during the summer and fall. When water is abundant, alligators move freely throughout the sawgrass marshes. During the dry season, alligators find or construct deep water holes, called gator holes, in which to seek shelter.

At night, alligators working individually use their clawed and webbed feet, tails and shovel-like snouts to excavate these sites. Their jaws are used to tear away vegetation. When finished, the gator pond may measure thirty feet across and three to four feet deep. The gator's stubby feet—with five digits on the front feet and four on the back—are excellent digging tools. Claws on the inner three digits of each foot aid its owner in climbing and digging.

In addition to their gator holes, alligators also dig horizontal dens or burrows into the muddy banks. These dens extend ten to twenty feet underneath a protective layer of soil and vegetation, and provide shelter during drought, excessive heat and winter cold. The tunnel entrance to the den is begun below the

waterline and ends above it in an air-filled chamber. Here, an alligator can retreat from the daily sun, or wait out the dry season should the water hole evaporate.

Crocodilians, like many other animals, appear to have a sophisticated navigational ability. When transported outside their home territory, juvenile American alligators appear to use short-term geomagnetic changes and celestial clues (solar, stellar and lunar) to find their way back home. When in difficulty, they seem to have a water-seeking orientation which quickly brings them to safety in the nearest river or lake.

Cypress swamp, Highlands Hammock State Park, Florida.

Several three- and four-year-old Louisiana alligators were able to return home after being tagged then relocated twelve miles away. Another made it back in three weeks after traveling eight miles.

Older gators appear to use multi-coordinate navigation, that is, the ability to detect at least two divergent large-scale geomagnetic gradients, one at their present location and another at their preferred destination. However they navigate, a one-eyed alligator traveled thirty-five miles in two weeks to return home to Nine-Mile Pond in Everglades National Park after being relocated.

The crocodilians' cost-effective metabolism aids them in all of their activities. It is undoubtedly an important aspect of their evolutionary success. When times are hard, unlike birds and most mammals, they can "shut down" and go for long periods without food. American alligators live in some of the coldest temperatures of any of the crocodile family. Like other cold-blooded reptiles living in temperate climates, alligators become inactive during the winter season, and seek an aquatic refuge from the dropping temperatures. In the loosest sense of the word, they "hibernate" for almost four months. During that time they rarely move and eat little or nothing. Some survive by lying torpid in the still water of large lakes.

Young alligator in the Everglades.

Unlike frogs, turtles and many other amphibians which can drop their metabolic rates low enough to exist on anaerobic respiration during winter hibernation, alligators need access to oxygen throughout the cold months. According to I. Lehr Brisbin, Jr., of South Carolina's Savannah River Ecology Laboratory, radiotelemetry studies of free-ranging adult alligators during winter showed that with the approach of freezing weather, large gators seek out shallow backwater areas. Here, with their nostrils positioned in such a way as to keep a small breathing hole open, they remain immobile as the ice forms above them. Even when their snouts become frozen in solid ice, the gators can survive brief periods of intense cold with no ill effects—as long as their breathing hole remains open. Such thermal inertia apparently only works for gators with large body mass. During extreme cold, juvenile gators seek protection in their mother's den.

Water Fluctuations

Water levels are critical to the well-being of alligators. High water can flood nests, and drought can lead to cannibalism when too many alligators are forced to share limited water real estate. Those that are squeezed out may dry out and die.

During the dry season, alligator holes often provide the only available sources of water. As the season progresses, they provide critical life support for frogs, turtles, water snakes, snails, shrimp and crabs, and young fish that would otherwise die. A parade of seasonal migrants visit the gator holes, as do predators such as bobcats, otters and raccoons in search of easy, concentrated prey. This banquet of fish and other creatures in the gator holes corresponds to the breeding season of wood storks, herons, egrets and other wading birds that need

the food to raise their young. And should the gator holes dry up, the exposed dead fish make easy pickings for a host of carrion feeders, including vultures, grackles and red-winged blackbirds.

Not to be overlooked is the fact that an alligator hole provides a steady source of food for its owner. However, because alligators are cold-blooded, they don't need much food, even less so in the winter. Unlike mammals, which require a steady source of calories for metabolic heat generation, alligators don't have this problem.

Scientists have discovered that a variety of plant species in the Everglades are consistently associated with gator holes. Dirt excavated to make the pond and construct the den forms a fertile bank around the gator hole in which seeds of willows, bays and cocoa plums easily germinate. In successional stages, the plants grow into trees which provide shelter and nesting sites for birds. Deep-water plant species such as alligator flag and pickerel weed also colonize gator ponds.

An informative, two-hour tram tour offered by Everglades park naturalists at Shark Valley takes visitors on a fifteen-mile loop road through the heart of the Everglades sawgrass country. The tram passes one alligator hole after another, making it easy to see the dramatic impact alligators have had on this unique ecosystem.

MANAGEMENT
EFFORTS

chapter 8

Alligators
in the
Florida
Everglades.

*C*rocodilian natural history and reproductive biology have proven to be ideal for professional wildlife management. As a renewable resource with considerable commercial value, many crocodilian species are now being managed for sustained utilization—that is, no more crocodilians will be harvested than can be replaced by the population's normal reproduction. Several organizations and management efforts are instrumental in this goal.

Research Origins

By the late 1950s, due to the practice of unregulated harvest, alligator populations had declined to the point where they were no longer a renewable resource. The Louisiana Department of Wildlife and Fisheries stepped in to begin an aggressive program to rebuild alligator populations and restore the species.

"At that time, very little was known about the life history of the American alligator," explains biologist Ten Joanen, affectionately known among herpetologists as the "father of alligator research." For thirty-two years he headed Louisiana's alligator research and management program for the Department of Wildlife and Fisheries. Accurate natural history information was needed if a successful management program was to be developed for the reptiles. The state chose the 80,000-acre Rockefeller Wildlife Refuge as the site at which to concentrate research efforts and gather data.

Every type of gator study possible was initiated at the refuge. Alligators were caught, weighed, measured, sexed and tagged. Many were tracked using radio-telemetry. According to

St. Augustine alligator farm, Florida.

Joanen, Louisiana spent a tremendous amount of state time and funds to study alligator biology.

A way to count and inventory alligators was developed based on this research. The scientists discovered that nesting females comprise about five percent of a healthy alligator population. By counting active nests easily visible during helicopter surveys, it is possible to extrapolate overall population numbers.

As part of this research effort, Louisiana also developed the serially numbered alligator tagging system which is used around the world today. Every gator that is harvested must be marked with a special tail tag that shows that the reptile was legally killed within specified harvest quotas. The tags are tracked via computer.

Crocodile Specialist Group

According to the Crocodile Specialist Group (CSG), carefully regulated wild hunts, the ranching of eggs collected from protected wild populations and the development of closed-cycle breeding farms are being used to accomplish

conservation goals. The economic benefits resulting from a rigorously controlled legal trade in crocodilian skins has not only reduced hunting and poaching pressure on wild populations, but has also provided powerful economic incentives to preserve these reptiles, as well as their precious wetland habitats.

The 350-member Crocodile Specialist Group, at the Florida Museum of Natural History, University of Florida in Gainesville, provides a volunteer network of experts to assess conservation priorities, develop plans for conservation and initiate actions needed for the survival of the world's twenty-three species of crocodilians. The group operates under the auspices of the Species Survival Commission of The World Conservation Union. The group also works closely with the Convention on International Trade in Endangered Species of Wild Fauna and Flora.

In 1971, when the CSG began its conservation program, all twenty-three species of crocodilians were endangered or declining in numbers. Twenty-five years later, nine species are now sufficiently abundant to support well-regulated annual harvests; another five are no longer in danger of extinction, but are not abundant enough to be harvested; and seven remain critically endangered. According to the CSG, no other group of vertebrate animals has undergone such a dramatic improvement in its conservation status.

The CSG is now focusing its attention on the seven most critically endangered crocodilian species. These include the false gharial *(Tomistoma schlegelii)* of Indonesia and Malaysia; the Philippine crocodile, *(Crocodylus mindorensis)*; the Siamese crocodile *(Crocodylus siamensis)* of Cambodia, Vietnam, Laos, Thailand and Indonesia; the Orinoco crocodile *(Crocodylus intermedius)* of Columbia and Venezuela; the Chinese alligator *(Alligator sinensis)* of the Yangtze River valley; the Cuban crocodile *(Crocodylus rhombifer)*; and the gharial *(Gavialis gangeticus)* native to India, Pakistan, Bangladesh, and Bhutan.

Two additional species are listed due to "insufficient data" on their status in the wild. They are the African slender-snouted crocodile *(Crocodylus cataphractus)* native to west and central Africa, and Morelet's crocodile *(Crocodylus moreletii)*, which occurs in the Atlantic regions of Central America from Mexico south to Belize and northern Guatemala.

The CSG is also working to help threatened populations of the more

abundant species, and to gain greater protection for all species in national parks and wildlife refuges.

Everglades
National
Park.

Carnivore Farms

Alligators have always been hunted for their skins and meat. In 1800, alligator skins were sold in the Miami area for seven dollars each. To help meet the current commercial demand for alligator skins and products, and relieve pressure on wild populations, chicken-fed alligators are now being raised on farms for harvest-like livestock.

In 1994, approximately 470,635 pounds of gator meat and 59,806 skins were legally harvested in Florida, both at the farms and through a carefully reg-lated wild alligator harvest. The meat is sold to restaurants and wholesalers for five to seven dollars per pound. The skins are sold to leather tanneries throughout

the world, at twenty-five dollars or more per foot. According to the World Wildlife Fund, the alligator's commercial potential can be fully appreciated when one realizes that an average alligator harvested in Louisiana measures about seven feet in length and provides about twenty pounds of deboned, defatted meat.

More than 150 large-scale sustainable-yield alligator programs are now being run in several states, particularly Florida, Texas and Louisiana. Florida has developed a comprehensive alligator farming, ranching, and trapping system that is sustained largely by tagging and license fees. The system allows for licensed egg and hatchling collection for ranching purposes, as well as limited hunting of wild adult animals.

American alligator, Florida Everglades.

Ranching involves the removal of alligator eggs or hatchlings from the wild. These animals are then reared in captivity and their skins are later exported. As part of operational agreements with state governments, ranching programs must return seventeen percent of their hatch-rate back to the wild each year. In sort of a Head Start program for alligators, the juveniles are released at slightly older ages when their chance of survival is increased.

Controlled Gator Hunts

Researchers discovered that limited hunting did not harm healthy alligator populations. In fact, it did the opposite. A controlled, sustained-yield gator hunt not only benefited the big reptiles, but all wetland wildlife—by providing an economic incentive for preservation.

Most of the marshland inhabited by alligators in Louisiana is privately owned. By enabling land owners to profit from the alligator hide trade, they are encouraged to preserve the marshes rather than drain them for pastureland or development. This not only safeguards the valuable habitat needed by alligators, but that of all other wetlands

wildlife as well, particularly the waterfowl that winter in the marshes.

Swamplands edge most of the entire Louisiana coastline. These huge stretches of prime alligator habitat make it possible for alligator populations to regenerate quickly. As a result, in 1972 alligator hunting was resumed in Louisiana. Each year, hunters are able to kill roughly 20,000 gators without significantly depleting the overall population. When possible, their harvest system targets the reproductively peripheral members of the adult population—namely males and quiescent females.

In 1988, one year after the American alligator was officially removed from the endangered species list, the Florida Game and Freshwater Fish Commission (GFC) scheduled an alligator hunt, the first since 1962, as a means to assess the reptile's rapid population growth. The season ran for the month of September, and was restricted to twenty-eight wetland areas around the state. The GFC concluded that a controlled hunt was the best way to protect alligators and their habitats. Profits from hunting licenses and tag fees help support alligator-management programs and population surveys. Profits from the legal sale of alligator skins goes directly to the permit-holding hunters.

Nuisance-Alligator Program

Although Florida wildlife managers were aware of the need for a nuisance alligator program in the 1960s, it wasn't until the mid-1970s, when the GFC received 5,000 or more annual alligator complaints that formal guidelines were established. The GFC started by defining their philosophical position: that for every nuisance alligator killed, the full commercial value would be realized. Methods to handle the problem gators were then tested and implemented.

In keeping with the goal of using alligator harvest revenues to support the species' conservation and management, the GFC developed a plan by which a nuisance alligator pays for its own removal. Contract alligator trappers are not paid directly by the GFC. Instead, they get to cash-out the meat and skins of the nuisance alligators they remove.

Habitat Protection

In the Southeast, almost every wetland to the foot of the interior mountains was once inhabited by alligators. While alligators no longer inhabit many of their former areas, including southern Virginia or central Arkansas, they can still be found in reduced numbers throughout much of their historic range. Today, the biggest remaining threat to this downlisted reptile is habitat loss.

Swimming through the Florida Everglades.

Wetland development often makes their protected recovery seem greater than it is. When swamplands are filled and developed, alligators are forced to move into more confined areas. The result is an increased alligator concentration, which makes the reptiles seem omnipresent—especially when found floating in backyard swimming pools. Because wetlands are distributed throughout Florida in small pockets, not only is it more difficult for alligator populations to regenerate, but they are more adversely affected by real estate development; which is continuing unabated as more and more people migrate to Florida.

The backwater swamps of the South are among the most productive inland ecosystems of North America. It is said that the extremely rich soils of Cajun Louisiana, called "black gumbo," can make a stone sprout. The country's largest system of backwater swamps borders the Mississippi River and its tributaries. The lower Mississippi once nourished thick stands of forested wetlands that encompassed 700 miles and stretched across seven states.

It is estimated that 300,000 acres of wetlands are lost each year in the United States. No other wetland system in North America has been as drastically reduced as the lower Mississippi River and its tributaries. Today, only 4.4 million acres remain of the original 21 million acres of bottomland forests. Those that have survived are badly fragmented. Mississippi's Yazoo Basin, Louisiana's Atchafalaya Swamp and Arkansas' Tensas Basin "Big Wood's" region contain the largest intact stands of original forest.

Everglades National Park.

Today, an estimated 750,000 alligators live in the swamps and marshes of Louisiana, and about one million in Florida. Loss of habitat continues to be a problem for gators, as is pollution. Alligator skin samples now show high levels of mercury contamination in south Florida. Carried in their prey, such pollutants become concentrated in predators, like alligators, at the top of their food chains.

Because they are of vital importance to the healthy functioning of their ecosystems, alligators are considered a *keystone species.* Not only do they control prey species, but their nesting behavior creates peat and directly benefits other endemic wildlife species, such as the Florida red-bellied turtle, which incubates its eggs in alligator nests.

The gator holes provide food and refuge for numerous species during the dry season. As earth movers and mound-builders, alligators also provide fertile soil for the growth of native vegetation.

According to the CSG, crocodilians play valuable roles in their wetland ecosystems. They selectively prey on fish species, increase nutrient recycling, maintain aquatic refuges for other wetland species during droughts, and keep waterways open. Therefore, loss of any crocodilian species represents more than just the end of these functions. It results in a significant loss of biodiversity and ecosystem stability.

LIVING WITH ALLIGATORS

*Alligator
and turtles
on the
Homosasis
River,
Florida.*

$\mathcal{S}$wimming through a flood-control canal
in Florida, a seven-foot alligator ends up waddling across the parking lot of a
Miami shopping mall. Another rests on the warm tarmac of an airport runway. At
a putting green, a big gator intimidates golfers with its slow tail-dragging, high-
walk across the grass. Gators snooze and dine in the lakes and ponds on the
University of Florida campus. Another is photographed climbing a four-foot
chainlink fence. It feels like an alligator invasion is underway.

A man-made fountain spouts an artistic water spray in front of a sleek con-
dominium complex in Naples, Florida. The tinted glass, pink cement, manicured
lawns and brilliant bougainvillea gardens seem an unlikely spot for a prehistoric
reptile. Yet there, floating in the small man-made pond just a few yards from the
main entrance is a big, six-foot alligator.

Positioned near the fountain, the gator's motionless, primordial presence
with armored, bony plates protruding through the water's surface is startling, if
not funny. It floats in stark contrast with its artificial twentieth century environment. Even so, this upscale gator looks strangely comfortable in the fash-
ionable setting—a bold testament to the reptile's remarkable adaptability. From
the Age of Dinosaurs to the Age of Florida Condominiums, nothing seems to
phase a crocodilian.

The condo gator displayed the species' usual indifference to people. By day,
alligators sun themselves on logs, or rest at water's edge. Motionless, they follow
movement with their unblinking dark eyes, but otherwise seem reluctant to move.
When approached within a dozen feet or more, they simply belly-slide into the
water and disappear.

Not to be taken for granted, alligators can react quite dramatically when threatened. In an instant, they can raise up on their short legs to lunge, threaten and hiss. In short bursts, they can run faster than a person on land—normally in retreat to water. If cornered, however, they may attack.

Alligators swing their massive heads from side to side like bony clubs, snap their jaws, and thrash their tails when confronted. They are notorious for sudden forward lunges to bite, and are quick to nail foes with teeth or tail. A startling gymnastics trick helps them avoid capture. Tucking their legs against their sides, they use their tail to hurl themselves like whirling dervishes into a series of fast, slippery rolls—not unlike the "death roll" used to subdue and drown prey underwater. It's a defense strategy that works.

Despite once-uncontrolled hunting and relentless wetland destruction, alligators continue to thrive along the densely populated Southeast coast. Good wildlife conservation programs, controlled harvests and increased efforts toward public education have helped. So has the reptile's tenacious ability to survive.

In the duckweed waters of Florida.

Encounters

While most people view the alligator's population recovery and delisting as an endangered species a conservation success story, not everyone is pleased. At times the presence of these large reptiles juxtaposed with people is inconvenient—at others it is potentially dangerous.

In 1994, Florida's GFC received 13,431 "nuisance" alligator complaints from state residents. Any alligator more than four feet in length that appears to have lost its natural fear of humans, or poses a threat to people or property, falls into the nuisance category. Five regional offices of the GFC handle all alligator complaints.

Because alligators are classified as a threatened species, they are protected by state and federal laws. Only representatives of the GFC are empowered to handle nuisance alligators. At present, about forty nuisance-alligator control trappers work under contract for the Commission. In 1994 they obtained permits to legally kill 4,632 nuisance alligators.

Florida's nearly 7,500 freshwater lakes provide ideal gator habitat. They also provide ideal recreational habitat for people. The state's warm climate has already attracted thirteen million people, with around a thousand more arriving daily. In addition, thirty-eight million tourists visit the "Sunshine State" each year. Wildlife experts point out that alligators have been around for

millions of years, long before the Neanderthals came and went, and *Homo sapiens* evolved. As sidekicks of the extinct dinosaurs, crocodilians are one hundred times as ancient as human beings. This means that we are invading the alligators' backyards, not the other way around.

Such close contact has caused occasional problems. Pet dogs are routinely snatched. In 1995, a dalmation was killed by a ten-foot alligator, and another was killed in front of its owner when a thirteen-foot, two-inch gator suddenly lunged out of an overgrown pond to seize the pet.

According to leading crocodilian researcher Kent Vliet, a charging alligator is an incredible phenomenon. It starts by swimming fast. As it builds up power, churning hard with its tail, its head begins to rise out of the water. In a final surprise burst, it lunges right out of the water with its front legs flat to its sides and its mouth wide open. During such a charge, the gator's entire head, shoulders, and about half of its body explodes out of the water. Undoubtedly, the dog near the pond experienced just such a charge, and was grabbed and dragged back into the water.

The GFC receives numerous reports of gator attacks on pets. According to Lieutenant Jeff Ardelean, regional nuisance alligator coordinator for the Everglades region, barking dogs often attract large gators. One of the more interesting calls his office received involved a nine-foot alligator. While out for a nocturnal stroll one night, the hungry reptile passed near a house, which set the resident dog barking. In bold pursuit of the dog, the gator used its head to break right through a house window. At 2:00 a.m., the alarmed owner called the Commission to report the gator's big head sticking through his window. By the time he got off the phone, the determined predator had bulldozed its way through the house wall right into the kitchen. A nuisance-alligator trapper and wildlife officer assigned by the Commission quickly responded to take care of the situation.

Alligator and nutria face-off in Louisiana.

Although such events are rare, brazen alligators occasionally cause problems for people. In Everglades National Park, a family was forced to jump on a picnic

table when a bold gator decided he wanted to join their party. In another incident, a woman lost her hand to an alligator while scrubbing a pot in a lake where she routinely fed the reptiles. According to Gary Stolz, former Everglades National Park ranger now with the USFWS, this incident illustrates an important point. "Alligators don't know a hand from a handout. They should not be fed."

In 1972, a sixteen-year-old girl wasn't as lucky. At dusk, as she stood cooling off in a picturesque cypress-ringed lake in Florida, an eleven-foot alligator silently stalked her. Gliding like a reptilian torpedo the final forty yards underwater, the gator attacked and killed her. It turned out that this alligator also had been routinely fed by people.

In 1975, a twelve-foot alligator mauled a wildlife biologist in the Oklawaha River. In 1987, a man water-skiing on a lake near Daytona Beach, Florida, had his ankle seized by an eight-foot gator.

A few years ago when a resident pulled into his driveway on Sanibel Island, Florida, he was happy he had a cellular car phone. A nine-foot alligator blocked his driveway preventing access to his house. Afraid that his wife would let their five-pound toy spaniel out the door to greet him, he used his car phone to warn her. Disaster was averted.

Education Reduces Risk

While man-eating reptiles may stalk and slither through our nightmares, in reality, American alligators rank pretty low on the list of dangerous fauna. Surprisingly, deer hold first place on the list of North American animals dangerous to man. About 130 people a year are killed by these big-eyed herbivores, mostly as the result of car collisions. The next most deadly creature is the bee, which kills roughly 43 people a year. Dogs (14), rattlesnakes (10), and spiders (4) follow, with jellyfish and goats ranked more deadly than grizzlies and mountain lions.

American alligators have a mixed reputation when it comes to aggression against people. Worldwide, it is estimated that crocodiles are responsible for the loss of about 2,000 human lives each year. In contrast, from 1973 through 1994, only 156 documented alligator attacks occurred on people in Florida— seven of them fatal.

Alligator impersonating a log in the Florida Keys.

The execution of wild animals that kill people seems to help satisfy the need for retribution among grieving family members and alleviate the resurgence of predatory fears triggered by such events. Sharks of all species have been the target for excess public emotions ever since shark attacks were so graphically portrayed in the movies. In Hawaii, vigilante efforts to kill sharks peak whenever a tiger shark attacks a surfer, body-boarder or diver. And it's not just sharks that pay the price. In July 1992, after two people were killed by bears in south-central Alaska, seventeen bears were killed as retribution in a single two-day period.

Often after a gator encounter, local residents press officials to destroy all alligators in the area. This would eliminate the legal liability that the wayward creature might strike again. It would also enable biologists to perform autopsies to learn why attacks occur. However, many believe the mass slaughter of bears, cougars, sharks or alligators following a human death is no solution to the problem of how to share space with such predatory megafauna.

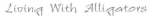

At the apex of their food chains, predators play a critical role as conservation managers. Their carnivorous diets help maintain healthy ecosys-tems. In an effort to dominate and destroy them, we often jeopardize entire ecosys-tems. When we invade their space, we literally put them at risk. Human error usually causes most fatal animal attacks. When such an attack occurs, the animal invariably pays with its life.

In short, we need to be educated, wary and respectful when we visit wilderness areas. The possibility of a rare animal attack is part of the thrill of being in the presence of such magnificent animals. When you enter their domain, you take that risk.

Toothy grin of an alligator in Avery Island, Louisiana.

HOW TO BEHAVE
IN GATOR
COUNTRY

chapter 10

Alligator nest in Everglades National Park.

A predatory beast nearly twice your size with inch-long teeth, prehistoric armor and a modus operandi of aggressive surprise definitely deserves respect. Unlike the man-eating estuarine crocodiles of Australia and Southeast Asia, and the Nile crocodiles of Africa, which will gladly gulp down a person as easily as an antelope, the American alligator definitely has a more benign reputation. Under most circumstances they would rather flee than fight. The problem is that people often become too complacent in the presence of these seemingly disinterested reptiles. And therein lies the danger.

During a visit to Okefenokee National Wildlife Refuge, my two sons suddenly decided to take a jar and catch tadpoles off the canoe rental dock. Dipping their hands in and out of the dark water, they quickly filled up the jar with tiny tadpoles, and began playing catch and release with them. Their fun had only just begun, when a ranger rushed out of the nearby building to ask them to get their hands out of the water. He explained that an alligator had grabbed a fisherman by the hand as he leaned over a nearby dock, rinsing his hands and gear in the water. The stealthy reptile had been attracted to the prey-like movement at the water's surface, and in crocodilian fashion had remained concealed until the moment of attack.

The tadpole incident illustrated why parents need to keep a watchful eye over children when visiting alligator habitats. Oblivious to the potential danger of attack, children spontaneously engage in the very activities that put them most at risk. Predators typically stalk prey that is vulnerable and distracted. Children match that profile.

Perfect camouflage in southwestern Florida.

In addition to human carelessness, the intentional feeding of alligators has caused serious problems. "If a gator abruptly comes up to me and stops," explains Everglades National Park naturalist James Laray, "it tells me it has been fed by people. Normally alligators are afraid of humans. Feeding breaks down these barriers, making alligators turn bold and dangerous."

Outside park boundaries, during a high-speed airboat ride over south Florida's famous river of grass, I had a chance to see just how bold human-fed gators can become. After gliding forward and sideways over the grass, the driver slowed down to explore the hammocks and deep-water channels—and to whistle. Conditioned to the sound of his voice, alligators suddenly materialized out of nowhere. Emerging from concealment to swim toward the boat, some swam so fast they created rooster-tail wakes with their powerful tails. What could cause such a response among these normally reclusive creatures?

It turned out to be marshmallows, which the boat driver from the private tour company tossed to each of the responsive reptiles. Rewarded for their close approach to the boat, the carnivorous gators showed more than one sweet tooth as they aggressively snapped up the floating sugar puffs. This human-caused feeding frenzy illustrated why it is not such a smart idea to provision alligators—or any wild animals. Feeding can turn normally shy reptiles into greedy, aggressive beasts that often trade their own lives as pests for short-lived human amusement. For this reason, Florida law prohibits the feeding of wild alligators, as does federal law inside national parks and national wildlife refuges.

Do's and Don'ts in Gatorland

Small alligators (less than four feet) pose little threat to people. They are still immature. The gators to avoid are those over four feet in length. The Florida Game and Fresh Water Fish Commission recommends the following safety tips:

- Never approach an alligator too closely. They are agile both in and out of the water.

- Avoid swimming in areas inhabited by large alligators, especially at dusk or at night when the reptiles often feed. Keep your children—and pets—out of these areas as well.

- Do not swim outside of posted swimming areas. When you do swim inside these marked areas, always swim with a partner.

- Avoid areas with thick vegetation along shoreline, as this is ideal habitat for large alligators.

- Do not feed alligators, this includes throwing fish scraps into the water or leaving them on shore.

- Supervise your children! Do not leave them unattended in wildlife refuges where alligators roam freely, or in back-yards bordering alligator habitat.

- Alligators assess their prey by its height. If confronted by an aggressive alligator, stand as tall as possible, even raise your hands above your head to add height.

- Because alligators feed on rotting meat, an alligator bite can result in serious infection. If bitten, seek immediate medical attention.

- Do not remove alligators from their natural habitats, or keep them as pets.

- Because it is illegal to kill or harass an alligator, call the Florida Game and Fresh Water Fish Commission to report a problem reptile.

- Texas, Louisiana, Georgia, Alabama, Mississippi and South Carolina also have nuisance alligator programs. They can be reached through the local state game and wildlife departments.

Alligators and turtles basking in the Louisiana sun.

A CONSERVATION SUCCESS STORY

Alligator in duckweed, L. Martin Swamp, Louisiana.

The reptilian order Crocodylia—crocodiles,

caimans, gharials and alligators—includes some of the most valuable and heavily traded species in international commerce. With hides unmatched in durability and appearance, the persistent demand for skins to supply an almost insatiable fashion market—and black market for poached crocodilian skins—eventually led to a world-wide species decline.

Fueled by human greed, vanity and consumerism, the extensive illegal crocodilian trade was so effective at wiping out wild populations that by 1967 the American alligator was added to the list of endangered species. Yet a year later, despite such protective listing, it was estimated that ninety-seven percent of all alligator goods in trade were still coming from illegal sources.

Tougher state and federal laws coupled with improved law enforcement and habitat management helped turn the alligator situation around, as did the development of a unique conservation model that balanced crocodilian biology with basic economics. In what could best be described as a "bio-economic" model for conservation, scientists figured out how to harness the forces that once drove the illegal skin trade—namely fashion, high consumer demand and profit—to drive conservation. They did this by developing management plans for alligator populations that viewed the reptiles as a for-profit, renewable resource.

Alligator's dorsal scutes, Florida.

The American alligator's conservation epic began in 1855 when tanners and manufacturers of leather goods in France discovered the beauty and durability of products made from their tanned hides. Overnight, alligator hunting in the United States went from sport to profitable adventure. While the Civil War slowed down overseas trade in alligator skins, it prompted renewed gator killing due to war-related food and leather shortages in the South. Gators were killed for their meat—their tail and jowls are said to taste like fish. Their skins were turned into leather, and their oil used to lubricate machinery in the cotton industry.

The pressure on wild alligator populations jumped another notch in 1870 when, closer to home, several American tanneries began processing gator hides. This marked the end of the era of large alligator populations first described by the early explorers and colonial settlers. Tannery records indicate that ten million alligator hides were processed between 1870 and 1965. The decade between 1881 and 1891 accounted for more than a quarter of them, when most of the large populations were quickly slaughtered. As supply decreased in the decades that followed, demand and prices for skins increased.

Between 1930 and 1940 an estimated one to two

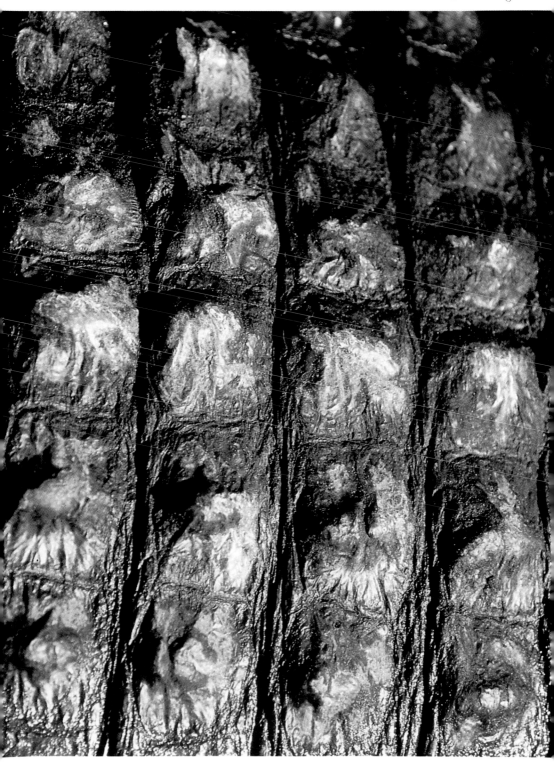

million alligators were killed in Florida alone. Such unregulated harvest took a devastating toll on the American alligator. This prompted imposition of the first state hunting restrictions in Florida, Georgia and Louisiana—but poaching continued.

Florida countered in 1962 by giving complete legal protection to the American alligator. That same year, Louisiana also closed its alligator hunting season, further reducing supply. But all this did was increase the prices and market demand for gator skins. A renewed rash of poaching and hide smuggling across state lines ensued, further decimating the wild populations.

Poachers killed alligators in protected park and refuge areas and hunted them from cars along roadside canals. Conservation officers and park rangers routinely discovered piles of alligator bones and skinned carcasses in the Everglades, but rarely the poachers. In 1969, two years after the alligator was officially listed as an endangered species, a report in the *Miami Herald* estimated that 250 poachers were making a full-time living by killing alligators illegally in the national park and surrounding wetlands. One such poacher reportedly cached his hides up and down Highway 41 which bisects the Everglades. After a night's work slaughtering reptiles, his partner would fly in at dawn, land on the highway, load up the skins, and fly to another state where they could legally be sold.

To put a stop to this, several additional laws were passed. Urged by conservationists, New York passed the Mason-Smith Act in 1969, which banned the sale of all endangered species and their products within the state. Connecticut, Massachusetts, Pennsylvania and California subsequently passed similar laws. By eliminating the U.S. market for illegally obtained hides, poaching began to decrease.

In 1970, Congress passed the Lacy Act, which prohibited inter-state transport of illegally taken wildlife. This made the interstate shipment of alligators and other wildlife a federal violation. With passage of the Endangered Species Act in 1972, penalties for poach-ers were increased. These measures gave justification for the Florida Game and Freshwater Fish Commission (GFC) to ask for increased funding to enforce the laws and prosecute offenders. So empowered, the GFC's strict enforcement of the poaching laws helped the American alligator recover. Population surveys initiated by the GFC in 1974 showed progressive annual population increases.

According to the World Wildlife Fund, the alligator program developed in the United States is considered the model wildlife man-agement and trade program. In fact, Louisiana's innovative conserva-tion program for alligators has provided a model for management and research around the world. As proof, Louisiana's current alligator populations are as high as—if not higher than—those which existed at the turn of the century. The majority of Louisiana's gator habitat and the largest segment of the alligator population are both found in the southern third of the state.

In turn, Florida has attempted to develop alligator population models as a means to set harvest quotas at maximum sustainable yield.

Such computer harvest models are appealing, but scientists now realize that harvest strategies need to be site-specific. Each harvest requires on-site evaluation both before and after implementa-tion. Often, socio-economic research on current market demands for alligator skins and meat can be just as important as the biological research on specific wild populations.

Soaking up the warmth of the Florida sun.

One thing is certain. By viewing an alligator as a com-mercial, renewable resource, rather than just a sacrosanct endangered species, everyone involved in the skin and leather industry has a vested interest in the reptiles' survival. Many companies not only contribute to conservation pro-jects, but actively work to help reduce illegal trade.

Unlike the majority of endangered species which are difficult to breed and have little commercial value except for their rarity, crocodilians, with their unique natural history and reproductive biology, have proven ideal for professional wildlife management.

Carefully regulated wild hunts, the ranching of eggs collected from pro-tected wild populations, and the development of closed-cycle breeding farms all contribute to the goal of sustained yield. The economic benefits derived from all management efforts provide powerful incentives to preserve not only the relic reptiles, but their precious wetland habitats.

Thousands of crocodilians continue to be killed each year for sport and commerce. Thanks to such conservation efforts, no modern crocodilian species has become extinct in the wild—yet.

WHERE TO SEE
ALLIGATORS
IN THE WILD

Appendix A

*M*any people consider the river swamps in the Southeast some of North America's last great wilderness. Here are a few suggested places to experience the country's best swamplands, alligators included.

Alabama

Bon Secour National Wildlife Refuge, located along Alabama's south coast near Gulf Shores, offers several good places to look for alligators. There are two hiking trails in the 6,200-acre refuge that access wetland areas inhabited by the reptiles. The four-mile Pine Beach Trail is a good place to look for alligators, as is Gator Lake. Most of Bon Secour's gators measure from six to twelve feet in length.

Alligators can be seen just about year-round at the 11,600-acre Eufaula National Wildlife Refuge located near Auburn in southeastern Alabama. According to refuge biologist Daniel Drennen, quite a number of them can be seen in most of the impoundment areas—a system of levees built for water management.

Anhinga Trail, Everglades National Park, Florida.

Roads built on top of the levees provide access and good visibility into the impoundment areas. The refuge can also be explored on foot and by boat. The best time to see alligators is during midday in the spring and fall, and early morning and late afternoon during hot summer days. The reptiles are least visible during January.

Wheeler National Wildlife Refuge, located in the north end of the state near Huntsville, also offers opportunities for the public to see alligators. It is possible to see gators in this 34,500-acre refuge at two locations—Blackwell Swamp, and at the gravel pits located behind the town of Moorseville.

Arkansas

Arkansas represents the northern extreme of the American alligator's natural range. As a result the reptiles are not abundant, nor easily seen. An estimated one hundred alligators inhabit the 65,000-acre Felsenthal National Wildlife Refuge. The refuge is located near Crossett, just north of the Louisiana border. According to refuge biologist Robert Ellis, the best time to see gators is from March to October when they sometimes bask on the banks of the Ouachita River.

The refuge contains more than 15,000 acres of permanent water, most of it in a series of backwater lakes. It is here that the alligators reside, making them difficult to see and census. The refuge staff has caught a ten-foot gator, and discovered a couple nests with hatchlings.

Florida

The Everglades, a shallow, fifty-mile "river of grass," is a vast, complex water system that flows from Lake Okeechobee south more than one hundred miles to Florida Bay. Once stretching nearly coast to coast, its 4.3 million acres contains a unique ecosystem of remarkable plants and animals found nowhere else on Earth.

The best time to explore the Everglades is in winter from November to April when the notorious mosquitoes and sandflies are least apparent. It is also the dry season, the best time to see the park's wildlife as it congregates around remaining water sources. During the rainy season, from May to November, the wildlife disperses as rainwater collects in the huge expanse of sawgrass and cypress trees. In November, the water begins to evaporate and in places the mud hardens and cracks. Many alligators retreat to centuries-old gator holes—damp tunnels clawed deeper than the parched rivers and drying sloughs. Others seek winter sanctuary in the remaining deep-water lakes and ponds, many near tourist trails and boardwalks.

In Everglades National Park, as many as two hundred alligators may gather at Shark Valley and Royal Palm by the end of the dry season. Shark Valley and the Anhinga Trail are the best places to view alligators in the park.

Alligators can also be seen in the Arthur R. Marshall Loxahachee National Wildlife Refuge in the northern Everglades. Here the Marsh Trail and Canoe Trail offer excellent viewing opportunities.

Alligator young in Florida.

Georgia

The popular Okefenokee National Wildlife Refuge straddles southeast Georgia and northeast Florida. Here, alligators dominate the landscape. Big and small, boldly sunbathing, or invisibly submerged—gators are everywhere. At night their eerie eyeshine animates a flashlight beam.

Encompassing 396,000 acres of waterlogged peat bog prairies, "The Swamp" is as appealing as its name. The prairies, in fact, gave the refuge its name. *Okefenokee* is a Creek Indian word meaning "land of the trembling earth." Step out onto any of the swamp's spongy habitat and the meaning becomes immediately clear.

Okefenokee is famous for its abundant wildlife, including black bears, owls, bobcats, deer, otters, raccoons, birds and gators. Designated a national wildlife refuge in 1937, the Okefenokee also provides habitat for the endangered wood stork, red-cockaded woodpecker, eastern indigo snake and gopher tortoise. Nocturnal, amphibious and aquatic, relying on camouflage and stealth to survive, many of the swamp's more interesting creatures are difficult to see.

The Okefenokee is a strange and wonderful place. A layer of peat up to fifteen feet thick rots beneath the surface of the tea-colored, lily-pad water. By analyzing the deepest layer of peat, scientists have determined that the Okefenokee peat has been rotting for almost eight thousand years. Tannic acid released from the peat gives the water its distinctive coloration, and name—"blackwater." The color has been described as "tea brewed strong enough to float a horseshoe." Gators not only cruise the shallow waters of the swamp but nest in the surface peat, utilizing the heat generated by the decaying plant material to incubate their eggs.

Hunts alligator ranch, Bushnell, Florida.

More than 300,000 people a year visit the Okefenokee, many to explore the estimated 120 miles of boat trails. Canoe rentals and guided day tours are offered by the Okefenokee National Wildlife Refuge. Several commercial outfitters offer a variety of camping trips and photographic workshops in the swamp during the spring and fall.

Louisiana

There are many excellent places to see alligators in Louisiana; among them is the 80,000-acre Rockefeller Wildlife Refuge located near Grand Chenier. It was here that biologist Ted Joanen initiated his pioneering research on the behavioral ecology of the American alligator.

According to Joanen, alligators spend a great deal of time sunning themselves as they come out of hibernation, making spring the best time to see them in the wild. Because coastal wetlands have made it difficult to build roads throughout the area, the best way to explore the numerous gator haunts of Rockefeller Wildlife Refuge is by boat. Private tour companies around Houma also offer swamp tours to see alligators.

Barataria Preserve, part of the Jean Lafitte National Historical Park and Preserve located in Marrero is another good place to look for alligators. It contains natural levee forests, bayous, swamps and marshes. Over eight miles of hiking trails, including two-and-a-half miles of boardwalk, allow visitors to explore the various environments. Nine miles of canoe trials, closed to motorized boats, and accessible by three canoe launch docks allow further exploration of the swamps and marshes. Alligators can be seen sunning along the banks, or sub-merged with only their eyes and nostrils showing. Ranger-guided walks and canoe treks are presented year-round. Canoe rentals are available just outside the preserve.

Alligators also inhabit the Atchafalaya River floodplain that flows for 140 miles south from its junction with the Mississippi River to the Gulf of Mexico. Larger than the vast Okefenokee Swamp of Georgia and Florida, Louisiana's Atchafalaya River Basin contains nearly one-half million acres of hardwood swamps, lakes, and bayous. Considered the nation's largest network of forested wetlands, America's Great River Swamp is located at the southern end of the Lower Mississippi River Valley in south-central Louisiana. Two of the best places to access this area are the 11,780-acre Sherburne Wildlife Management Area and the adjacent 15,220-acre Atchafalaya National Wildlife Refuge.

Alligators can also be found in the Delta National Refuge located along the southeastern coast of Louisiana, on the Mississippi River delta. Established in 1935 to provide winter sanctuary for migratory waterfowl, the refuge encompasses 48,800 acres of marsh, shallow ponds, channels and bayous. During some years, up to 200,000 migratory ducks (eighteen species) and 50,000 snow geese pass the winter months here. Alligators can be spotted year-round. The ponds and bayous provide good gator habitat.

American alligator in duckweed pond, Avery Island, Louisiana.

Located just forty miles north of New Orleans is Bogue Chitto National Wildlife Refuge. Much of this 37,000-acre refuge, situated on the Louisiana/Mississippi border, is accessible only by boat. It encompasses bottom-land hardwood forests and a series of bayous, oxbow lakes and main river systems that provide ideal habitat for alli-gators, as well as 166 species of birds.

Bayou Sauvage National Wildlife Refuge is located just twenty minutes from downtown New Orleans. *Bayou Sauvage*, which means "natural waterway," is one of the largest urban wildlife refuges in the country. The 22,770-acre refuge is located entirely within the corporate limits of New Orleans in Orleans Parish. This unique refuge offers wetlands of several types, access to the city's canal and pump station system, and bird wintering and nesting grounds and islands.

"Take a drive on just about any coastal road through southern Louisiana," advises biologist Ruth Elsey with the Rockefeller Wildlife Refuge, "and you can see alligators floating in every ditch."

Mississippi

According to Randy Breland, deputy project leader at Yazoo National Wildlife Refuge near Hollandale, it is easy to see gators during the spring, summer and fall. "We have large numbers of the reptiles," states Breland. "At one location in the refuge I was able to count twenty-nine alligators in just twenty minutes."

Yazoo National Wildlife Refuge is located in the heart of Mississippi's delta region, thirty miles south of Greenville. The refuge encompasses 12,941 acres of undulating Delta soils. One of the best places to look for gators is at Alligator Pond, which is easily accessible by car. From the parking lot, it is a short walk to the pond levee, which provides a good gator-watching overlook. Visitors can also access the Alligator Pond Nature Trail, which provides opportunities to see the reptiles along both sides of the trail. Green Tree Reservoir and Deer Lake are also good places to look.

Hillside National Wildlife Refuge, located just north of Yazoo City, is also a reliable place to scout for gators. It is possible to drive along the west levee to look down into a series of borrow ponds, bayous and slews inhabited by the large reptiles.

North Carolina

"Only two to five alligators at most are counted each year during an annual survey conducted at Swanquarter National Wildlife Refuge," explains refuge biologist John Stanton. "North Carolina represents the northern extreme of their range, and this is reflected in the few numbers that we see. Occasionally a stray gator may venture into Virginia, to be seen briefly, then is gone."

A much-publicized ten-foot alligator inhabited the canals at Mattamuskeet National Wildlife Refuge up until three years ago. The refuge is located in eastern North Carolina in Hyde County, about four miles northeast of Swanquarter NWR. Lake Mattamuskeet, the largest natural lake in North Carolina, is a shallow body of water that averages only two feet deep. Eighteen miles long by about six miles wide, its 40,000 acres of water take up most of the 50,180-acre refuge. This would seem ideal habitat for alligators, yet winter temperatures can occasionally dip below twenty degrees Fahrenheit, and on rare occasions the lake may freeze.

Oklahoma

Alligators occur infrequently in Oklahoma; it is the extreme northern limit of their range. One seven-foot alligator was caught on district land in 1982. Alligators are occasionally seen in the Red River bordering Texas, and in Little River National Wildlife Refuge bordering Arkansas; and every once in a while an alligator shows up in a pasture pond. Such gators, says refuge biologist Bill Long, are released into Little River NWR, but are usually not seen again. In other words, Oklahoma is not the best place to go in search of alligators.

Gliding through Florida waters.

South Carolina

One of the best places to consistently see alligators in South Carolina is the Cape Romain National Wildlife Refuge, located twenty miles north of Charleston. The 64,230-acre refuge stretches for twenty-two miles along the state's coast. During springtime, alligators can be seen sunning themselves along the banks of Jacks Creek impoundment and Upper Summerhouse Pond on Bulls Island. In fact, most of the refuge's gators inhabit the freshwater ponds and impoundments on Bulls Island, but occasionally a gator will venture onto the beach or into the saltwater surf.

Bulls Island lies nearly three miles off the mainland and is reached by boat from Moores Landing. A private ferry service takes visitors to the island on regularly scheduled days. Drinking water, food and insect repellent must be brought as there are no tourist facilities on the island. The six-mile-long, two-mile-wide island has sixteen miles of roads open for hiking and a two-mile national recreational trail. The only provisions on the island are restrooms and picnic facilities and an emergency weather station.

From a 1994 survey, it is estimated that Bulls Island is home to over six hundred American Alligators, some averaging more than ten feet long.

"Spring and early fall are the best times to see them," says Walt Rhodes, alligator project supervisor with the South Carolina Department of Natural Resources (SCDNR). "Along one section of the dike on Cape Romain, it is not uncommon to see seventy to one hundred alligators lined up sunning themselves."

Ace Basin National Wildlife refuge is part of the 350,000-acre Ashepoo, Combahee, and South Edisto (ACE) Rivers Basin. It is one of the largest undeveloped wetland ecosystems remaining on the Atlantic Coast. The 11,019-acre refuge has two separate units, one along the Edisto River and the other along the Combahee River. Alligators can best be seen in the refuge impoundments or managed wetlands areas because they support the highest densities of the reptiles.

According to Donny Browning, refuge manager for the ACE Basin National Wildlife Refuge, the alligator population in South Carolina is high. Alligators can be found in the coastal swamps and marshes throughout the state.

The 8,048-acre Donnelley Wildlife Management Area, located just south of Green Pond, is another good place to see gators. Managed by the SCDNR, the area encompasses a diversity of wetland and upland habitats typical of the coastal Lowcountry. Donnelley WMA is open Monday through Saturday from 8 a.m. to 5 p.m. Visitors are asked to be observant when walking due to the presence of poisonous snakes, and to remain on the dikes as the water levels adjacent to the dike roads are often very deep. It is illegal to feed or harass the alligators.

Similar instructions apply when visiting the 12,000-acre Bear Island Wildlife Management Area, located sixteen miles southeast of Green Pond. Here, as in many of the ACE Basin's old rice fields, alligators sun on the banks or float partially submerged.

Basking in the sun of Sarasota County, Florida.

Rhodes also recommends these additional locations to see alligators in South Carolina: the Savannah National Wildlife Refuge, located six miles south of Hardeeville; Huntington Beach State Park near Myrtle Beach, where alligators can easily be seen in a large pond near the entrance to the park; the 25,000-acre Santee Coastal Reserve; and the more inland Santee-Cooper Lakes area, including Santee National Wildlife Refuge where alligators inhabit the many cypress-studded sloughs.

Texas

There are several places along the Gulf Coast of Texas that offer good views of wild alligators. Aransas National Wildlife Refuge is one. Nearly surrounded by water, the refuge is located on Blackjack Peninsula, just thirty-five miles northeast of Rockport. In addition to alligators, the refuge is home to 392 different species of birds, including the whooping crane which is considered one of the rarest birds in the world. Established in 1937, the refuge has a sixteen-mile loop road for self-guided auto tours, more than six miles of hiking trails, an observation tower, and a visitor center. Ringed by tidal marshes and broken by long, narrow ponds, Aransas encompasses 54,829 acres. Although alligators live in freshwater, they can sometimes be seen feeding in the bays.

Located ninety miles east of Houston at the southeastern tip of Texas, McFaddin National Wildlife Refuge contains one of the most dense populations of American alligators in the state. Eight miles of interior roads provide excellent wildlife viewing opportunities and give access to inland lakes and waterways. Boat launches are also available. Depending on water conditions, however, inland lakes may be navigable only by canoe or shallow draft boats as they rarely exceed a few feet in depth. Alligators are most easily seen at McFaddin NWR during the spring, but are often visible throughout the summer and fall.

Alligators are also abundant in Anahuac National Wildlife Refuge located on East Bay. Main roads through the refuge can accommodate buses and recreational vehicles. Twelve miles of graveled roads provide opportunities to observe marsh wildlife. Visitors are welcome to walk on designated roads and trails, but are cautioned to watch out for poisonous snakes, fire ants and alligators. Plan ahead when visiting this refuge, as no gasoline stations are located on or near the refuge.

Everglades National Park.

At Brazoria National Wildlife Refuge located ten miles east of Freeport, Big Slough and other brackish and freshwater areas provide habitat for many species, including American alligators. Six miles of gravel roads course through a wide variety of wildlife habitats, providing opportunities to observe wildlife and to learn about marsh ecology. Due to limited facilities, access to the refuge is somewhat limited.

Finally, even Houston offers convenient opportunities to view alligators at Brazos Bend State Park. Nearby, Beaumont offers gator viewing at Big Thicket National Preserve. In fact, the place has been nicknamed "Gator Park" for the dozens of toothy reptiles that live there.

SELECTED READING

Appendix B

Alderton, David. *Crocodiles and Alligators of the World*. New York: Facts on File, 1991.

Aronsky, Jim. *All About Alligators*. New York: Scholastic, Inc., 1994.

Bothwell, Dick. *The Great Outdoors Book of Alligators and Other Crocodilia*. St. Petersburg, FL: Great Outdoors Publishing, Co., 1962.

Brook Van Meter, Victoria. *Florida's Alligators and Crocodiles*. Miami: Florida Power and Light, 1992.

Carmichael, Pete and Winston Williams. *Florida's Fabulous Reptiles and Amphibians*. Tampa, FL: World Publications, 1991.

Glasgow, Vaughn. *A Social History of the American Alligator*. New York: St. Martin's Press, 1991.

Hermes, Neil. *Crocodiles: Killers in the Wild*. Brookvale, NSW, Australia: Child and Associates Publishing Pty., Ltd., 1987.

Lauber, Patricia. *Alligators: A Success Story*. New York: Henry Holt and Company, 1993.

McIlhenney, Edward. *The Alligator's Life History*. Lawrence, KS: Society for the Study of Amphibians and Reptiles, 1987.

Ross, Charles and Stephen Garnett. *Crocodiles and Alligators*. New York: Facts on File, 1989.

Steel, Rodney. *Crocodiles*. London: Christopher Helm, 1989.

Toops, Connie. *The Alligator: Monarch of the Everglades*. Homestead, FL: The Everglades Natural History Association, Inc., 1979.

Toops, Connie. *The Alligator: Monarch of the Marsh*. Homestead, FL: Florida National Parks and Monuments Association, Inc., 1988.

Webb, Grahame, Charlie Manolis and Peter Whitehead (eds). *Wildlife Management: Crocodiles and Alligators*. Chipping Norton, NSW, Australia: Surrey Beatty and Sons PTY Ltd., 1987.